THE RED DR
&
THE WEST WIND

THE RED DRAGON
&
THE WEST WIND

The Winning Guide to Official
Chinese & American Mah-Jongg

TOM SLOPER

Collins
An Imprint of HarperCollinsPublishers

HarperCollins books may be purchased for educational, business, or sales promotional use.
For information, please write: Special Markets Department, HarperCollins Publishers,
10 East 53rd Street, New York, NY 10022.

FIRST EDITION

Designed by Helene Berinsky

Library of Congress Cataloging-in-Publication Data

Sloper, Tom
The Red Dragon & the West Wind: the winning guide to official Chinese & American
Mah-Jongg / Tom Sloper.
p. cm.
ISBN: 978-0-06-123394-4
ISBN-10: 0-06-123394-3
1. Mah-jongg. I. Title.

GV1299.M3S56 2007
795.3'4—dc22   2006051897

HB 05.08.2023

CONTENTS

INTRODUCTION

Playing card games and board games with my family while growing up in upstate New York in the fifties and early sixties, I had no idea I was training myself to become a designer and producer of video games and computer games. And I didn't know what mah-jongg was back then. Fast-forward to the 1990s. I had just returned from working for several months at Activision's Tokyo office, and was assigned to produce the Super Nintendo and Sega Genesis versions of Shanghai II: Dragon's Eye. The Shanghai series had been very successful for Activision—they regarded it as an "evergreen" title, a game that could be updated and rereleased every couple of years. For nine years, I was "Mr. Shanghai." I enjoyed the simplicity and purity of the tile-matching game, but as time went on, as the Internet became a force in games, it became clear to me that for the next new version, Shanghai needed to include the actual game of mah-jongg.

I began to study up on mah-jongg. I bought two books. And right away I was confused. The two books were both about mah-jongg, but the books described games that were different from each other. I soon learned that there were multiple variations on the game. I bought a computer game, Hong Kong Mahjong, and started practicing the Hong Kong Old Style variant. And that was the beginning of a long love affair. Since then, I've played in Hong Kong, Japan, Europe, China, and, of course, here at home in the United States. Through my participation in

Internet forums and newsgroups, I came to write the Mah-Jongg FAQs (answers to frequently asked questions) and a weekly column, both of which I host on my Web site, Sloperama.com. I've learned a lot in the process.

I'm not the greatest player in the world. I wish I'd started learning at a younger age, and had been playing mah-jongg longer. I enjoy collecting information about as-yet-undiscovered variants, and about the history of the game. I play American mah-jongg weekly, and I don't play Mahjong Contest Rules (Chinese Official) mahjong often enough. I love meeting players from around the world. I have mah-jongg friends all over the planet, and I wouldn't trade them for the number one spot at a tournament.

This book is a labor of love. And it's just the tip of the iceberg. The strategies outlined in this book are all well known among other players and authors. It's up to the individual reader to build upon them and create a winning strategy all his or her own.

It's exciting to see the momentum building. Poker has opened the door for other games to be televised. And have you listened to *Sunday Puzzle with Will Shortz* on National Public Radio? He's always traveling to some puzzle competition somewhere in the world—sometimes exotic and far-flung locales. Mah-Jongg is poised to attain greater heights in this century than it did in the last, and it's going to be a wonder to behold.

Tom Sloper
Los Angeles, California, USA

1

HISTORY OF MAH-JONGG

Ancient Times

Many other books and articles on mah-jongg, going back to the 1920s, refer to mah-jongg as an "ancient" game, supposedly thousands of years old. Some authors even said mah-jongg was enjoyed as a favorite pastime of Confucius. Truth be told, mah-jongg, contrary to popular belief, is *not* thousands of years old. Mah-Jongg actually originated in the mid- to late 1800s, probably in the vicinity of Ningbo, China. It is believed that Chen Yumen, an officer serving during the time of the Taiping Rebellion, invented the game we now know as mah-jongg, based on previously popular card games and domino games.

The Chinese really did have games in ancient times. Dominos (which may have originated in Egypt) existed as early as 1355 B.C. The game of Go may have existed as early as 479 B.C., when Confucius's disciples compiled the Analects of Confucius. *Xiang qi* ("Chinese chess") may have existed as early as 203 B.C. (or it may have originated around A.D. 100, around the same time that a precursor to Backgammon, Ludus Duodecim Scriptorum, originated in Rome). The oldest written documentation of chess indicates that chess (or a precursor game) originated around A.D. 600 in India or Afghanistan.

So it's possible that Confucius (who died in 479 B.C.) may have enjoyed some game or other. But none of the games mentioned above resemble

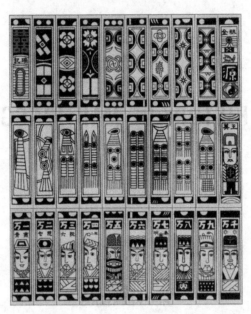

Chinese money-suited cards

mah-jongg in the slightest. The earliest definite reference to card games in China date back to A.D. 1294. Sometime in the twelfth century the popularity of cards supplanted the popularity of previous dice games in China. Those dice games had been referred to as *yeh-tzu*, and, after this time, for a while, China's card games were referred to by this name as well.

Those early Chinese cards were money-suited: the suits were Coins ("Cash"), Strings of Coins ("Strings of Cash"), and Lots of Strings of Coins ("Myriads of Cash"). Several different games evolved over the years, one of the most popular being *ma tiao,* a trick-taking game for four players, played with four-suited money cards. The composition of a *ma tiao* deck and the gameplay of *ma tiao* differ significantly from the composition of a mah-jongg set and from the gameplay of mah-jongg. Eventually, three-suited money cards became favored (one of the four money suits was dropped), and in a development that surely led to mah-jongg, a game known as *peng he pai* used quadruplicated three-suited cards (a full deck was 120 cards).

Playing games with suited cards was very popular in China. The prevailing theory is that cards traveled westward along the Silk Road, migrating to Islamic regions and thence to Spain during the Middle Ages. (An opposing theory has it that the cards originated in Persia, then migrated east to China and west to Egypt, and from Egypt north to Italy and the rest of Europe.)

The cards of the Islamic regions are now referred to as *mamluk* cards. The Middle Eastern Middle Ages was the era of the *mamluk*—slave soldiers who became a powerful military class (equivalent to the *samurai* of feudal Japan). In Europe, the cards became tarot, which led directly to our modern-day playing cards used for games like rummy, solitaire, canasta, bridge, and poker.

Mamluk *suit cards*   *Tarot suit cards*

In each region, the look of the cards was altered to suit local tastes. In *mamluk* cards and in tarot cards, the suits were Coins or Pentacles (Coins), Polo Sticks or Wands (Strings of Coins), Cups, and Swords. Those in turn migrated through German and French suit systems and became today's Diamonds, Clubs, Hearts, and Spades, respectively.

Meanwhile, as the card suits were evolving in the West, they were also evolving in China. Coins became Dots; Strings of Coins became Bams; Myriads of Coins became Craks. So you see, playing cards and mah-jongg are cousins, descended of the same ancestor—Chinese money-suited cards such as those used to play *ma tiao* and *peng he pai*. The fact that mah-jongg descended from those ancient card games does not make it correct to say that mah-jongg itself is "an ancient game," any more than it would be correct to say that mah-jongg's cousin, gin rummy (played with cards descended from *mamluk* cards and tarot cards), is "an ancient game."

The Nineteenth Century

During the time of the Taiping Rebellion, it is believed that Chen Yumen took quadruplicated money-suited cards of *peng he pai*, added extra pieces such as the four winds and the Red Dragon (among some other tiles no longer present in mah-jongg sets today), and, rather than using paper cards, had the symbols carved onto domino-like tiles. This Chen Yumen origin theory is the one espoused by the mah-jongg museum in Ningbo today. The Display Hall of the Birthplace of Mahjong is located at 74 MaYa Road, Ningbo 315010, China (Tel. 0574-8729-3526).

J. B. Powell wrote in his article "Mah Chang: The Game and Its History" (*China Weekly Review*, June 30, 1923) that General Chen was not the only person whose contributions to mah-jongg could be documented; Powell credits Chang Shiu-Mo, also of Ningbo, with adding flowers and seasons to the set.

The games that until then had been played with money-suited cards, like the European game of tarot, were mostly trick-taking games. So Chen Yumen may not have created just a set of tiles. He seems to have also initiated a new way of playing with them. Or perhaps he borrowed it from card games.

The game mechanic of making a full hand of complete sets in a turn-based game that involved picking and discarding seems to have come into existence around the middle of the 1800s.

The ancestor of today's rummy games was called *conquian*. It's a Spanish name, and the game seems to have originated in the Philippines or Mexico. From Mexico, *conquian* migrated into the southwestern United States, expecially Texas, where the name became Americanized into "coon-can."

British card-game writer and historian David Parlett notes that the 1920s American card-game writer Robert F. Foster "traces Conquian back to the early 1860s." It is not known at this time which game, mah-jongg or conquian, came into existence first. It may be that Chen Yumen's new way of playing migrated to the Philippines and Mexico, and was adapted to European playing cards . . . or possibly vice versa.

The earliest documented mah-jongg set (c. 1873).

According to mah-jongg historian Michael Stanwick, in his 2004 articles in *The Playing-Card* (the journal of the International Playing-Card Society), the earliest documented mah-jongg set (or tiles that most closely resemble the game now known as mah-jongg) dates to 1873 (see illustration above). This set doesn't have any Green Dragon tiles. Instead of four flowers and four seasons, the set has only four seasons (outlined in green octagons). The set includes four special "ruler" tiles: Heaven, Earth, Man, and Peace, and four directional ruler tiles: East, South, West, North. The 1873 set also included four extra blank white tiles (not shown here).

It is not known what Chen Yumen called his game, or how the game that was played with those early tiles differs from the classic style of playing that became popular in the twentieth century. Those unknown rules are sometimes referred to by mah-jongg historians as "proto-mahjong."

The Twentieth Century

Mah-Jongg's popularity in China blossomed after 1911 when the Manchu (Qing) Dynasty fell. To put things into historical perspective, 1911 was when Sun Yat-sen was elected president of the China Republic, the Kuomintang Party came into power, the Chinese calendar was reformed, and pigtails were finally abolished for men. Before 1911, mainly the elite, not common folk, had played the game. That changed after 1911.

An American oil executive, Joseph Park Babcock, was working in his company's Shanghai operation just after World War I. There was at that time a large community of foreign businessmen and their wives living in Shanghai, and the Chinese game then known as 麻雀 (*ma que* or *ma qiao*) became all the rage among these expatriates. Incidentally, among the foreigners living in Shanghai during that decade were a large number of Jewish refugees. It is probably safe to assume that at least some of the Jewish folks learned to play mah-jongg while taking refuge in Shanghai.

Intrigued by this addictive game and noting its incredible popularity among the foreign community, Babcock decided that the game would also catch on in America.

Babcock's "red book," softcover (L) and hardcover (R)

But, he reasoned, the tiles would need to be marked with Roman letters and Arabic numerals, since Americans would not be able to understand the Chinese characters. Furthermore, he saw some of the rules as being in need of a little simplification.

Babcock commissioned the manufacture and shipment of mah-jongg sets, trademarked the name "Mah-Jongg" (with hyphen and double *G*), and wrote a set of simplified rules. His rules were printed and bound in red covers, and included in sets imported into the United States in 1922 by W. A. Hammond's Mah Jongg Sales Company of America, in San Francisco.

The game's sales took off like a rocket. The venture succeeded beyond Babcock's wildest dreams. To understand why, we need to consider the times. This new Chinese game called "Mah-Jongg" had appeared on the scene when the American populace was very open to new experiences; new ways to have fun. The Roaring Twenties had just begun.

The decade of the 1920s was marked by a new cultural phenomenon: the fad. The 1920s saw the advent of flappers, the Charleston, Art Deco, speakeasies, and bootleg liquor. Music was getting more commercial, more danceable, more jazzy; and everybody could have music in their own homes as a result of phonographs, phonograph records, and player pianos. Silent movies were a new cultural phenomenon.

Society was more than happy to find diversions to help them forget the horrors of World War I and the horrific flu epidemic. They had been through interesting times, and survived. Young men no longer had to go to war. Young women, finding their way into a new position in society, were now wearing scandalously short dresses, cutting their hair short, wearing makeup, smoking cigarettes, and . . . playing mah-jongg. From its beginnings in America, mah-jongg was popular with the ladies. Young women are often the trendsetters in a society. In the case of mah-jongg, the role of the women was important early on. Everybody was playing mah-jongg. It was one of the hip fads of the day.

By 1923 Babcock's Mah-Jongg game became so popular that other companies also began importing and/or manufacturing, and selling, mah-jongg sets. And other authors wrote their own rule books. Because Babcock had trademarked the name "Mah-Jongg," these other companies had to use other names. They called the game Mah Chang, Pung Chow, Pe-ling, Chinese Tiles, the Game of a Hundred Intelligences, the Ancient Game of the Mandarins; and, thanks to Robert Foster, Mah Jong (with no hyphen, and only one g) became

widely accepted as a generic name that didn't violate Babcock's trademark.

Babcock had made alterations to the Chinese rules to simplify them for American players. This simple act was to have tremendous implications for the evolution of the game in America. Babcock's competitors went to China to research the rules. Mah-Jongg, or so it seemed, was played slightly differently in different parts of China.

Mah-Jongg, the hot new game! (Not to mention the babes!).

Babcock's competitors found these different rules, and especially they reinstated details that Babcock had omitted, and introduced them to America and Europe. Soon different books and articles disagreed on basic principles of the rules, and soon the wars were raging.

Skillful players became desirous of the chance to go for the big score, and were tired of being thwarted by novice players who just went for the cheap quick win. New table rules (the One Double Game and the Cleared Hand Game) were favored by the skilled players, while novices preferred the simpler Mixed Hand Game. These preferences clashed mightily. For American mah-jongg, the 1920s turned into the "Raging Twenties."

With these conflicting ways of playing, it was not long before the players got into rules disagreements when playing with others who used different rules. With so many different authorities, it was more and more difficult to obtain a coherent solution to conflicts.

So, as happens with all fads, the craze began to ebb.

Just a few of the many mah-jongg books of the 1920s.

In 1924, in an effort to cork the dike, five of the most influential mah-jongg writers at the time (M. C. Work, Robert F. Foster, Joseph P. Babcock, Lee Hartman, and J. H. Smith) banded together as the Standard Rules Development Committee. The result was a unified set of National Standard Mahjong Rules. The Cleared Hand, One Double, and Mixed Hand games were all acknowledged as legal options to be played at the discretion of the players at a particular table.

STANDARDIZATION COMMITTEE OF THE AMERICAN OFFICIAL
LAWS OF MAH-JONGG

But it was a case of too little, too late. The new standardized rule system still didn't do much to boost the sagging popularity of mah-jongg, especially as far as male players were concerned. The Roaring Twenties
ended, the flapper dresses were put in mothballs, and the Great Depres-
sion ensued. Gradually, the male authorities (and thus male players)

dropped out of the mah-jongg business. The rules confusion still prevailed, primarily because there was no governing body, the committee's influence not lasting very long.

Robert F. Foster wrote a book, *Twenty-Point Mah Jong*, which created yet another way to play. Flowers, Foster suggested, could be used in the hand, rather than melded instantly and replaced. This not only heaped more dirt on the grave of Chinese Classical, but also helped pave the way for the American variant. This novel way of using flowers sparked the imagination of female players who wanted to keep on playing mahjongg, but were unsatisfied with the complexity of the classic game.

THE NATIONAL MAH JONGG LEAGUE

From the point of view of the American women who still enjoyed the game, the men had messed things up pretty good. Now it was time for the women to take charge.

American women loved the tiles but didn't care for the mathematical nature of the classic Chinese game. They started creating fun hands composed of sets of like tiles, abolishing the "chow," a sequential run of numbered suit tiles (akin to the runs in rummy). Thus grew the concept of "pretty patterns."

"Lucky Lindy" commemorated Lindbergh's 1927 cross-Atlantic flight.

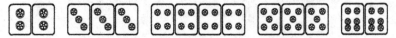

A "pyramid" hand from an early NMJL card.

This new concept caught on, and women traded hand ideas with their friends and relatives who still played. But this new way of playing had a flaw. Because there was no national authority, each group had its own list of hands. It was hard for a player to join another group, since she quickly had to come up to speed on their special hands—and adjust her strategy accordingly.

So in 1937, four ladies in New York—Viola L. Cecil, Dorothy Meyerson, Herma Jacobs, and Hortense Potter—decided to form a national organization. The National Mah Jongg League (NMJL) was established to standardize rules, and to publish a standard list of hands on a printed card that would change from year to year. The first president of the league, Viola L. Cecil, wrote the rules into a book of rules and an explanation of the card, entitled *Maajh, The American Version of an Ancient Chinese Game*.

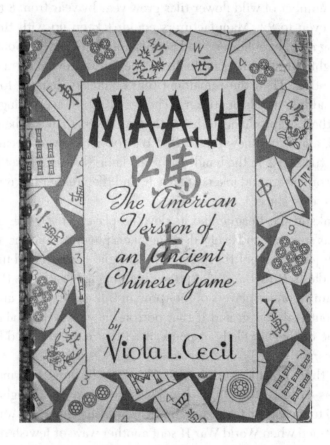

In the interest of keeping the game fresh, the League tried different things with the card each year. Each year, the card had special hands devoted to the year of the card. Flowers (and seasons, too, all lumped together and called "flowers") were now used as wild cards.

These features appealed to the female players. The League's card caught on with women in the New York area, and then spread up and down the eastern seaboard and soon across the continent of America. Rather than a game for couples to enjoy together, it became a "ladies' night out" pastime. During World War II, the NMJL rule cards were emblazoned: "Proceeds donated to patriotic and charitable causes." After the war, the patriotic causes were dropped, but the charitable causes were still championed.

The number of wild flower tiles grew year by year from 8 to 12 to 16 and even to 22. Manufacturers couldn't keep up with the ever-changing number of flowers, and neither could the players. Some players bought two sets and cannibalized one set to provide extra flowers for the other. Then the remaining tiles could be changed to flower tiles by adding decals or stickers. Then, in 1961, to keep things interesting, the League changed the use of the flowers to make them regular tiles, and added new tiles called Big Jokers. Flowers became just another tile to use in the hand. Ten years later, the League settled the number of flowers and jokers at 8 each, and the number has remained the same ever since.

Thanks to the League and its devoted players, the game of mah-jongg has survived and evolved, rising like a phoenix from the ashes of the mah-jongg wars of the 1920s. The League has survived until the present day, setting the rules and maintaining its position as the leading organization for players of the game in this country. Ask an American about mah-jongg, and if that person knows anything about the game, he or she will likely respond, "Isn't that a game played by Jewish ladies?"

And there is some truth in that. The Jewish connection may have begun as early as the 1910s when Jewish refugees in Shanghai were exposed to the classic Chinese game. The Jewish connection was probably fortified when World War II sent another wave of Jewish refugees to Shanghai, where mah-jongg was still highly popular. And the new NMJL game having begun in New York, it surely spread to Jewish neighborhoods of that city during the war. These factors may help explain why American mah-jongg is still popular in Jewish circles. Some people today think of American mah-jongg as "Jewish mah-jongg," but when one considers that perhaps 60 to 70 percent of the players are Jewish, 98 to 99 percent of them are female, and 99 to 100 percent of them are American, it seems more appropriate to think of it as "American."

As for the perception that many players of American mah-jongg are older, this too has a basis in fact. When this modern American game began to be played, it was played not just by older women, but by women of all ages.

What happened to the game of American mah-jongg? The 1960s. Mothers expected to involve their daughters in the game, but their daughters became more interested in burning their bras, dropping out, and turning on. The women's lib movement oddly further estranged daughters from mothers. So new young players stopped joining the games during the turbulent sixties. By the seventies and eighties, mah-jongg was seen by young women as a game for their elders.

The tide turned again in the 1990s, when the young women of the sixties, now grown up, saw their kids striking out on their own. Empty Nester syndrome prompted the now-reformed bra-burners to seek sociable pastimes, and mah-jongg became a reasonable option. The growth of the Internet provided them with a way to learn the rules, to get answers, and to find other players. The American game was growing again, and finding a receptive audience among ever younger players.

CHINA

Meanwhile, back in China where mahjong had been born, other changes had taken place.

The classical game's flaws were recognized not only in the West but also in the East. The classic method of scoring that had caused "wars" in America was recognized to be far too complicated. Regional variants emerged, notably the Cantonese game (also known as Hong Kong Old Style). These variants were used primarily for gambling, and most went undocumented entirely. A few have been documented only recently.

China's Cultural Revolution strongly discouraged gambling or the hint of gambling. Mah-Jong was driven underground. The Cantonese game, which survived due to Hong Kong's status as a British colony until 1997, was well established by the 1960s. Largely similar to the classical game, it utilizes a greatly simplified scoring system.

Under the philosophy "If you can't beat 'em, join 'em," it was decided to establish a set of legal rules for mahjong. These rules would not involve money but rather be played for sport, for ranking in a "mind sports" type of competition.

In defining the new official rules, mahjong research was done on China's regional variants, in Shanghai, Hong Kong, Beijing, Ningbo, Tianjin, and even Taiwan and Japan. It was decided that a pattern-based style of play, with simple additive scoring, would be created. Thus in 1998 the Chinese Mahjong Competition Rules (CMCR) saw the light of day, thanks to the People's Sports Publishing House.

These rules were used first in 2002 in Tokyo, Japan, at the first ever World Championship of Mah-Jongg. The championship was originally to be held in Ningbo, the city of the game's birth, but it turned out that Ningbo couldn't host the event. Takeshobo, a publisher of mahjong comic books in Japan and owner of the Mahjong Museum in

Chiba, Japan, took up the flame and organized the event in Tokyo. Competitions were held to qualify players from China and Japan. Players from other nations were invited to attend, and Ruth Unger, the president of the National Mah Jongg League, was an honored guest. One hundred players competed for two days in a heady Olympic-flavored phenomenon.

The author (R), Tokyo, 2002.

That historic event was followed by Chinese national competitions in 2003, 2004, 2005, and 2006 (Hainan, Hong Kong, Beijing, and Tianjin, respectively) and a European competition in 2005.

Following the 2005 competition in Nijmegen, Netherlands, the European Mahjong Association was formed, and it was decided to hold a follow-up event in Denmark in 2007.

In Beijing in 2005 the World Mahjong Organization was formed. It was decided to continue refining and improving the rules and to hold the second World Championship in Beijing in 2007 (following the Danish event). With the creation of this international committee, the new Chinese Official rules are now poised to become the international standard. If they aren't already.

The Twenty-first Century

The future of the American game depends on two things. The NMJL must keep doing what it's been doing—creating a well-balanced new card each year in a way that keeps the players engaged. And the game needs to keep bringing in new young players. And indications are that this is what's happening. There is an American-style tournament happening somewhere in the United States (or on a cruise ship not far offshore) just about every week of the year.

But for international competitions, the official Chinese rules are where it's at. Asian cultures are seen today as open and accessible. People travel freely to Japan, China, and other parts of eastern Asia where mah-jongg is played. Young Americans are becoming interested in Asian culture, thanks to Japanese and South Korean animation and video games. Young people of Asian heritage attend American colleges where they introduce the game of their homeland to their white-bread friends. Mah-Jongg is no longer just a game for old folks.

Regional and traditional variants are not about to die out. Their adherents will continue to enjoy playing mah-jongg the way they always have. Players of different variants can coexist in harmony. Players of different variants can pick up the official Chinese rules and join in the competitions.

There is a trend recently to consider certain table games like Go (*wei qi, baduk*), *xiang qi* (Chinese chess), chess, backgammon, and now mah-jongg, as "mind sports." It's likely that mah-jongg's visibility will be increased through a growing awareness of mind sports in general. Poker has recently become a televised competition. Mah-Jongg is tremendously popular as a televised competition in Japan, and as international competitions continue and gain the public eye, mah-jongg's future is looking bright.

2
MAH-JONGG BASICS

The classic Chinese game of mahjong took the world by storm in the Roaring Twenties. Since that time, many styles have evolved, some now more important than others. Two of the most important variants are Chinese Official mahjong and American mah-jongg, the forms that are the focus of this book. Since both games come from the same roots, they share many characteristics: essentially the same tiles, setup, and deal. Additionally, the play of both games is largely similar. The Chinese Official game uses "chows," runs of three sequentially numbered suit tiles, and an unchanging list of scoring patterns; flowers are not used in the hand itself and score extra points if the hand is won. The American game uses jokers and flowers in the hand, and a list of scoring patterns that changes every year.

A. The Set of Tiles

To learn the game of mah-jongg, it's important to begin by learning about the tiles of the mah-jongg set. Whether playing American rules or Chinese Official rules, the set is the same. The only difference is that the American set adds eight joker tiles.

The mah-jongg set consists of three suits, plus some extra nonsuited tiles. The three suits are called Dots (or Circles), Bams (or Bamboo), and Craks (or Characters). Each suit consists of tiles numbered 1 through 9, quadruplicated. The remaining tiles are the winds, dragons, flowers, and, for American mah-jongg, jokers.

If you own a mah-jongg set, I recommend that you open it now and organize the tiles as shown in this chapter. Whenever you purchase a new set, you should examine and organize the tiles prior to playing, because sometimes the manufacturer may have included extra tiles, and because variations in tile designs warrant familiarization.

THE THREE SUITS—DOTS, BAMS, AND CRAKS

We're all familiar with playing cards, with their four suits of Hearts, Diamonds, Spades, and Clubs. So, too, do mah-jongg tiles come in suits. American players call the mah-jongg suits Dots, Bams, and Craks. Whereas in playing cards, the suits consist of a single set of cards numbering from 1 (ace) to 10, plus some face cards, in mah-jongg, the suits are made up a little differently.

Mah-Jongg suits number from 1 to 9, and there are four of each numbered tile in the suit.

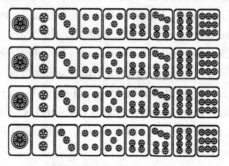

The suit of Dots (Circles)

Above: the suit of Dots. Each tile depicts a number of circular designs, corresponding to the tile's place within the suit. Some refer to this suit as Circles, Wheels, or Coins. The Chinese call this suit *tung* or sometimes *bing*.

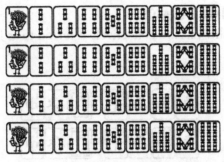

The suit of Bams (Bamboo)

Above: the suit of Bams, short for "bamboo." The "one bam" tile usually depicts a bird: sometimes a peacock, sometimes a sparrow or crane. Each other tile in the suit depicts a number of bamboo sticks, corresponding to the tile's place within the suit. The Chinese name for this suit is *tiao*.

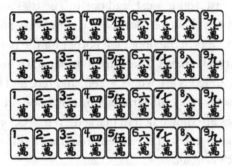

The suit of Craks (Characters)

Above: the suit of Craks. Each tile depicts a Chinese number, corresponding to the tile's place within the suit. The black Chinese character at the top of each tile is a number from 1 to 9, and the red character at the bottom of each tile is the number 10,000. Some refer to this suit as Characters or Ten Thousand, or by the Chinese name for this suit, *wan*.

The three suits consisting of 36 tiles each add up to 108 tiles. The number 108 has significance in Buddhism, and in Hinduism as well. The number 108 has been called "sacred" and "mystical," and the specifics needn't be examined here.

THE HONORS—WINDS & DRAGONS

The winds and dragons are collectively referred to as honor tiles or just "honors."

The Winds   *The Dragons*

The four winds correspond to the four cardinal directions of a compass or map: east, south, west, and north. The tiles are emblazoned with the Chinese characters for these terms. Westernized tiles also have Roman letters in the upper left corner for the benefit of players who cannot read Chinese. There are four of each wind tile.

The three dragons are white, green, and red, and there are four of each. Because many illustrations in this book are in black and white, the tiles are shown herein marked "Wh," "G," and "R." But it often happens that actual tiles are marked with different letters—or with no letters at all.

Players in China do not actually call the dragon tiles "dragons"—that is a Western practice.

THE FLOWERS & JOKERS

Unlike the suit tiles and the honors, which all come in fours, there are eight flower tiles. And, in the American set, eight joker tiles.

Flowers   Jokers

The flower tiles come in a variety of designs. In one set, the eight flowers usually look different from one another. The flowers in one set don't necessarily look like the flowers in another set. Flower tiles may be marked with the names of seasons (SPR, SUM, AUT, WIN). In some sets, flower tiles might depict people, or animals, or buildings, or objects. Flower tiles are almost always marked with the numbers 1 through 4. And flower tiles often have small Chinese characters on them (usually the names of the seasons or flowers or objects depicted). In this book the flower tiles are usually shown marked with a letter "F."

The numbers on the flowers had importance in the old classical game, but this feature has been done away with in many modern variants. When playing American mah-jongg or Chinese Official mah-jong, the numbers and writing on the flower tiles can be ignored.

VARIATIONS

Because mah-jongg sets come in a variety of styles, you might find it challenging to identify your tiles based on the illustrations in this book. So a word of explanation is in order.

One Bams

One Bams vary from set to set. At right: the 1B used in this book.

The One Bam tile is usually depicted as a bird. On some antique mah-jongg sets, you might observe a different design. If you have four bird tiles in your set, those are your One Bams. Especially if they're marked with a number 1.

Dragons

The dragon tiles in many American sets incorporate pictorial representations of dragons, rather than the Chinese characters seen on Asian sets.

Dragons as depicted in this book.

In this book, because the illustrations are in black and white, the White Dragon tiles are marked "Wh;" the Green Dragon tiles are marked "G;" and the Red Dragon tiles are marked "R." But actual dragon tiles are usually marked differently.

Various White Dragons you might encounter.

The White Dragon might have a rectangular design, or it might be blank. The letter "B" stands for *bai-ban* ("blank tile"). The letter "P" stands for *po* ("white"). Older mah-jongg sets (and sets made in Japan and Korea) use blank tiles for the White Dragon. American players came to call this tile "soap," accordingly. In American mah-jongg, the white dragon is sometimes used to represent zero in numerical patterns. If your set has four tiles with rectangular designs or four blank tiles, those are your White Dragon tiles. If you have both four rectangle tiles and four blank tiles, choose which ones you want to designate as your White Dragon tiles, and leave the others in the carrying case.

The Green Dragon is often marked with the letter "F." The tile may depict a green-colored dragon design, or it might be marked with the Chinese character *fa*. In Chinese, *fa* means "get rich"—thus Western writers usually refer to it as "fortune."

Various Green Dragons you might encounter.

The Green Dragon might or might not look like any of the above designs. If you have four green tiles that don't belong to a suit, or four green tiles marked "F," they are your Green Dragon tiles.

Various Red Dragons you might encounter.

The Red Dragon might look like one of the above, or might be some other design in red. The letter "C" stands for *chung* ("center"). If you have four red tiles that don't belong to a suit, they are your Red Dragon tiles. The Red Dragon is often marked with the letter "C". The tile may depict a red-colored dragon design, or it might be marked with the Chinese character *chung*. It's the national symbol for China (the central nation; the center of the world).

Flowers

Flower tiles come in many different varieties. Novice players, faced with an unfamiliar set of tiles, often find themselves confused as to whether or not a particular tile is a flower or not. As a general rule of thumb, if a tile isn't a wind, isn't a dragon, isn't a suit tile, and isn't a joker, then, everything having been eliminated, it must be a flower. It's common to mistake a one bam tile for a flower. As a general rule of thumb, if it doesn't have a beak or wings, then it's a flower. There are sometimes exceptions, since each set is different. This is why it's a good idea to inspect and organize the tiles as shown in this chapter.

Typical flower tiles (season tiles are flowers).

Some flower tiles depict flowers, and have numbers and season names written on them. Some flower tiles depict objects or people, and have numbers or wind designators written on them.

Some alternate flower tiles.

Some flower tiles depict animals.

"Animal" flower tiles.

The preceding tiles depicted are all flower tiles! This is why I recommend that when you get a new mah-jongg set, you lay it out as shown in this chapter. Once you have identified all your suit tiles, your winds, dragons, and jokers, then the leftover tiles are probably your flower tiles. Many American mah-jongg sets come with extra flowers, jokers, and sometimes blank tiles. Now you know how to identify your tiles.

Jokers

The joker tiles in one American set often differ from the jokers in another set. The joker tiles in your set are probably marked with the English word "joker," but not always. Some players have their names engraved on their joker tiles. Because not all mah-jongg sets come with joker tiles, some players apply stickers to create jokers.

American
Joker

Chinese
Joker

Some sets come with Chinese joker tiles and a booklet that incorrectly refers to those tiles as White Dragons. The tile shown here is inscribed with the Chinese words, "100 Uses." The character for "100" looks a little like the character for "white," and the writer of that booklet simply made an error.

If your set doesn't have 152 tiles, then it can't be used to play American-style mah-jongg. It is possible to find replacement tiles, but it may be easier simply to get an American set.

PUT IT ALL TOGETHER—THE BIG SQUARE

Arranging the tiles to form rectangles of the Dots, Bams, and Craks as shown previously, and a fourth rectangle of the winds, dragons, and flowers, the tiles can be laid out to make a square, as shown below. Thus, it's easy to see that the number of winds, dragons, and flowers equals the number of tiles in one suit.

Each suit is 36 tiles (9 times 4). The number of winds, dragons, and flowers is also 36.

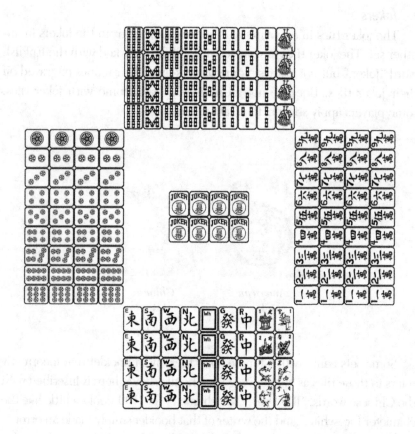

Above: a set of tiles for American mah-jongg: 152 tiles. Take away the eight jokers, and you have a Chinese mahjong set.

Again, I recommend that you organize your own tiles just as you see above, so you can compare yours with the illustrations in this book, and become familiar with the variety that exists between mah-jongg sets.

B. Additional Pieces

American mah-jongg sets come with additional accessories: racks, chips, dice, and wind indicators ("bettors"). Chinese mahjong sets may come with nothing but tiles, dice, and a wind indicator.

American-style racks (with chips), "bettor," and dice.

Racks are used by American players to line up the walls, push out the walls, hold the hand tiles, and display the exposed tile groupings. Some racks come with chip holders at the left side.

Most players use coins (quarters, dimes, and nickels) to settle up after a hand, but sometimes it's more prudent to keep score with chips.

A pair of dice is needed to break the wall at the beginning of each hand. Many sets come with very small dice. Lots of players prefer to buy bigger dice (available at drugstores or toy and game shops).

Wind indicators were originally created to keep track of game progress, but this usage has been lost in the American game. They may still be used that way in the Chinese Official game. When Americans play with a fifth player who acts as "bettor," the wind indicator can sometimes be used to indicate which player is being bet on.

C. Setting Up

Mah-Jongg is often played as a home game, with one of the necessary four players hosting the game. To play mah-jongg, a well-lit area is needed. Ideally, the table should be no smaller than 33 inches square and no larger than 36 inches square (83 to 91 centimeters square). A standard card table is the perfect size.

In addition to the four chairs, it's a good idea to have some small tables nearby for players to put drinks and snacks on.

When players arrive to the play session, it's customary to have the set already out of its case and on the table, so you can immediately begin playing.

When you are ready to begin, take all the tiles from the case and then turn them facedown, mixing them thoroughly. You all then work together to build the walls.

Chinese players build walls that are two tiles high and eighteen stacks long. American players build walls that are two tiles high and nineteen stacks long, lined up along the backs of their racks.

Chinese walls are eighteen stacks long, slightly angled.

Building randomly mixed facedown tiles into walls is akin to the practice in card games of shuffling the deck. It adds the factor of chance into what tiles the players will receive, and the dealing procedure prevents cheating.

American walls are nineteen stacks long (lined up using racks).

D. Dealing

The deal works essentially the same in all forms of mah-jongg. In the Chinese Official game, dice are rolled to determine the seating arrangement and who will deal first. In American mah-jongg, players sit where they like and the hostess is the first dealer of the evening's session.

The dealer rolls dice to determine where to break the wall. In the Chinese game, an additional roll takes place. Without going into details that differ between the two games, let's assume that the wall break is determined to be at the ninth stack. The dice are removed from the center of the table and placed at the dealer's right.

The dealer makes a break in the wall after the number of stacks specified by the dice. The tiles to the right of the break will be remaining where they are. This is the back end of the wall. The deal commences with the tiles to the left of the break (clockwise from the break).

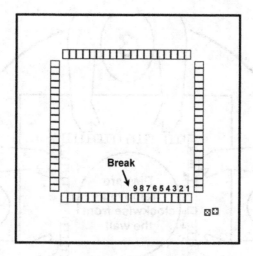

The dealer takes the first two stacks (4 tiles) to the left of the break.

Then, the player at the dealer's right takes the next two stacks (4 tiles). The player across from the dealer takes the next two stacks. The player at the dealer's left takes two stacks.

This continues, with each player taking two stacks, until all players have taken two stacks three times. Each player now has 12 tiles.

Note that although players are taking turns counterclockwise, the tiles are removed from the wall in a clockwise direction.

To finish up the deal, the dealer will take 2 more tiles, and the other players all take 1. The dealer takes the top tiles from the first and third stacks. Then the player to the dealer's right takes the end tile. Then the player across from the dealer takes the top tile from the end stack. Then the player at the dealer's left takes the end tile.

Now the dealer is holding 14 tiles, and all the other players hold 13 tiles. Each player arranges the tiles in the hand to begin playing. Chinese players stand the tiles on end; American players line up the tiles on the sloping front of the rack.

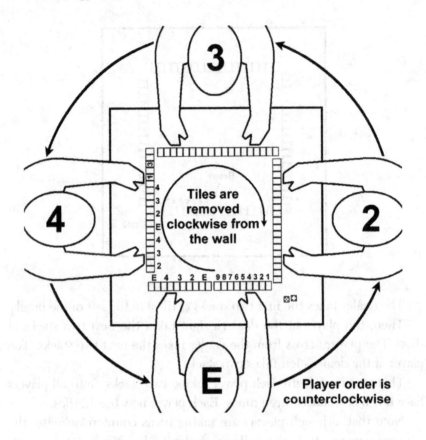

E. The Play

Mah-Jongg is a four-player game, in which each player competes against all the others. There are ways for fewer than four or more than four to play, but the game is best when played with four.

The goal of mah-jongg is to be the first to form a complete hand of 14 tiles. On each player's turn, the player will bring a fourteenth tile into the hand, either by picking it from the wall or by taking someone's discard, then (if the hand is not yet complete) discard one faceup in the center of the table.

Mah-Jongg is played similarly to the card games of the rummy family. The winning hand will usually be composed of a number of sets of tiles that form a pattern of some kind. See some example patterns, following.

Chinese Hand: "All Evens"

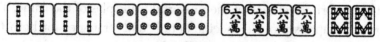

American Hand: "2468"

Chinese Hand: "Big Four Winds" and "All Honors"

American Hand: "Winds-Dragons"

Most Chinese hands are made up of four sets and a pair (per the above examples), while the structure of an American hand can vary greatly. When a player's tiles are dealt at the beginning, the tiles usually don't clearly suggest one particular hand. Experienced players see numerous possibilities and then may keep multiple possible hands open as incoming tiles shape the hand.

As play progresses, each player in turn picks and discards a tile to try to build a complete hand. Mah-Jongg combines luck and skill. The luck is in the deal and in the tiles picked from the wall. The skill is in choosing which tiles to discard.

During the course of play, players are permitted to call for discarded tiles only under certain circumstances. Only the most recent discard may be used; all other discards are considered "covered" once a new discard appears. A discard may not be taken unless it can be used to complete a set of tiles—such as a pung for instance—and the set completed by a discard must be exposed for all to see.

When a player declares mah-jongg, the game stops. The winner exposes the completed hand for verification of the players, announcing the score. In American mah-jongg, nonwinners pay the winner in chips or coins. In Chinese Official mahjong, the winner might collect chips or points on paper. Only one player can win a hand of mah-jongg! Then the players throw in all their tiles, which are then shuffled and built into a new wall for another game.

That's a brief overview of the universal principles of the game. The following chapters provide specific details and strategies for both the American game and the Chinese Official game.

3

AMERICAN MAH-JONGG

The American rules were first codified in 1937, in order to create a unified set of rules for American players. Although I call these rules the "American rules," this is only to differentiate this style of playing from the other styles. Other authors may use the term "American" to refer to other variants of the game.

The American rules are governed by the National Mah Jongg League, in New York City. The league refers to the game as "Mah Jongg" (as two words, with no hyphen and with two Gs). But the name originally given the game by Joseph Park Babcock in 1920 is hyphenated, so that spelling is used throughout this chapter.

The American rules are subject to updates and improvements by the National Mah Jongg League. The rules are available directly from the NMJL, and I recommend that the reader obtain those rules for a thorough understanding of the game. This book introduces the basics of the official game, and offers strategy tips above and beyond the rules themselves. If you are already familiar with the game but need a quick refresher on the rules, you may wish to refer to Section A of this chapter.

Distinguishing Characteristics of American Mah-Jongg

It is estimated that 98 or 99 percent of American players are female. The reason for this is that the American game was created by women, to suit the tastes of female players. The American game is all about using sets of identical tiles to make eye-pleasing and/or logical patterns. And chatting between hands. And kvetching, lots of kvetching. And laughing and enjoying a game together for a few hours each week.

A significant difference between this form of mah-jongg and other forms is the fact that American mah-jongg changes every year, with the publication of a new card that defines and limits the hands that can be made. Changing the hands each year keeps the American game fresh and challenging.

Another significant difference from other variants is the American game's absence of chows (sequences of three numbered suit tiles, such as 1-2-3, or 6-7-8). American mah-jongg hands are made solely of groupings of identical tiles—singles, pairs, pungs, kongs, quints, and sextets.

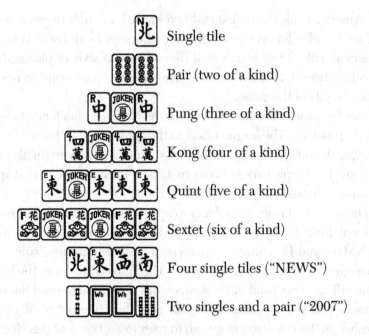

Although there are just four of any particular tile in the mah-jongg set (excluding the flowers and jokers), it's possible to make a set of more than four of a kind because jokers may be used to complete the set.

The use of sets of identical tiles (without numerical sequences such as chows) makes the American game less mathematical than all the other forms of mah-jongg. But it's one of the most challenging forms to learn and to master.

Dragons are suited in American mah-jongg. The Green Dragon belongs to the suit of Bams. The Red Dragon belongs to the suit of Craks. The White Dragon belongs to the suit of Dots (except when used as zero).

It isn't difficult to see that the Bams are mostly green, and that there is red on every Crak tile, but some new players have difficulty making a connection between Dots and white. Think of the suits as precious stones. Bams are green jade; Craks are red rubies; Dots are pearls. Pearls are round like dots, and pearls are white like the White Dragon tile.

Jokers may be used only in pungs or kongs or greater—never in a pair or to represent a single tile. Flowers are used within the hand, to make sets. These and other basic rules are always printed directly on the back of the NMJL card.

It will add to your understanding and enjoyment of this book if you have an NMJL card for reference. For information about how to obtain the card, see Appendix 2.

The card itself is the primary means by which the league keeps the game fresh. By issuing a new card each year, with a different list of hands, the league keeps the players challenged and stimulated. Among all the different ways mah-jongg is played around the world, the American game is unique.

A. Rules of American Mah-Jongg

This is a thorough statement of the rules, without illustration. A more detailed explanation of how to set up and play, with illustrations and examples, is given in Section B of this chapter. This section is good to bookmark or photocopy for novice players, or to answer sticky questions.

American mah-jongg is governed by the National Mah Jongg League, who may issue changes to these rules. The rules stated here were written based on the rules as publicly defined by the NMJL as of 2006. If any difference is found between the rules stated here and rules as stated by the NMJL (either in the official rule book, on the back of the card, or in the yearly bulletin), the NMJL rules hold sway.

THE TILES

1. The game is played using a set of 152 mah-jongg tiles, the standard 144-tile Asian set plus 8 joker tiles.
2. The 144-tile Asian set consists of suit tiles, honor tiles, and flower tiles.
3. The three suits, called Dots, Bams, and Craks, consist of tiles numbered from 1 to 9, each number quadruplicated within the suit. Thus there are 36 tiles per suit, for a total of 108 suit tiles.
4. The honor tiles consist of 4 different wind tiles, N, E, W, and S, each quadruplicated, and 3 different dragon tiles, white, green, and red, each quadruplicated. Thus there are 16 wind tiles and 12 dragon tiles.
5. The 8 flower tiles typically are decorated with images of flowers, and consist of 4 tiles marked in Chinese with flower names and 4 tiles marked with season names, but may instead be decorated with images of people, animals, buildings, vehicles, or objects, and marked with Chinese characters that tell a story. Flower tiles may be marked with numbers. The images, markings, and numbers on flower tiles have no significance in play. They are all simply called "flower."
6. The 8 joker tiles may or may not be labeled "joker" and may depict anything that clearly indicates that they are special tiles, used differently from the other tiles of the set.

THE TABLE AND PLAYERS

7. The game is played by four persons, each one competing against the other three, not partnered. Occasional friendly assistance of an opponent is permissible, but collusion is forbidden.

8. If a fifth player is present, that player may act as "bettor," if so determined by the hostess and other players.

9. The game requires a table, no smaller than 33 inches (83 centimeters) square and no larger than 36 inches (91 centimeters) square. A round table of 36 inches (91 centimeters) is acceptable. There must be four chairs suitable for the table, as well as accommodation for the players' refreshments (so that no food or drinks are on the table itself).

10. Each player at the table must have a properly licensed, properly obtained copy of the official NMJL card for the current year. Photocopies or facsimiles of the NMJL card are illegal and are subject to censure by the other players. Each player's card is placed on the table in front of the player and tucked beneath the player's rack.

11. There must be a pair of cubical dice, for use in randomly selecting the place where the wall shall be broken, so as to prevent cheating.

12. It is customary and expected to have a rack for each player. Racks are used for private viewing of one's hand, for lining up and serving one's wall, and for melding one's exposures. Racks may also have provision for retaining one's chips, if used.

13. If the players are playing for money, each player should bring to the game a purse containing coins amounting to the previously agreed total, or "pie." If playing in a public space where gambling would be frowned upon, chips are needed for exchange at the conclusion of each hand. If chips are not used, paper and pencil are needed to keep score.

14. There are various ways the first dealer ("East") may be selected.

    a. In a game played in someone's home, the hostess is customarily given the honor of first deal.

    b. When a game is played in a neutral location, players may each roll dice to determine who shall deal first, high roller taking that honor. In case of a tie, tying players roll again until the tie is broken.

   c. In a tournament, the tournament organizer designates which player shall deal first.

THE DEAL

15. The players shuffle the tiles facedown, then each player builds a wall, two tiles high and nineteen stacks long. Each wall is lined up behind each player's rack, forming a "great wall" in the shape of a square.

16. Dealer rolls two dice to determine where her wall will be broken. If after rolling, one or more dice lie outside the area bounded by the walls or do not lie flat, one or both dice (as reasonably deemed necessary) are rolled again.

17. The total number shown by the two dice is counted, right to left, from the right end of the dealer's wall. A break is made in the wall after (to the left of) the stack indicated by the dice, so that the number of stacks to the right of the break matches the number shown on the two dice.

18. The dealer herself takes 4 tiles (two stacks) after (counterclockwise from) the break and places them facedown on the table between her rack and the table edge (resting atop her NMJL card).

19. The player to the dealer's right (counterclockwise from the dealer) takes the next 4 tiles (two stacks) continuing clockwise from the break in the wall, and places them facedown on the table in front of her. Each player, taking turns counterclockwise around the table, takes 4 tiles (two stacks) continuing clockwise around the wall, until each player has taken thrice (is holding 12 tiles).

20. The dealer now takes the top tile from the first stack on the end of the wall, and the top tile from the third stack from the end of the wall, so that she is now holding 14 tiles.

21. Each nondealer player, taking turns counterclockwise around the table, now takes 1 tile from the end of the wall (the player to dealer's right taking the end tile, then the player opposite the dealer taking the top tile, then the player to the dealer's left tak-

ing the end tile). Each player who is not the dealer is now holding 13 tiles.

22. Each player may now examine her tiles, arranging them on the sloping face of her rack so that she can see the tiles but no other player can see them. She should organize her tiles by number, suit, and type in any fashion that helps her strategize the hand about to be played.

THE OBJECT OF THE GAME

23. The object of the game is to be the first to form a complete hand listed on the current NMJL card.

THE CARD

24. The card is issued each year on or about April 1. Thus the 2007 card is the card proper for use from April 2007 until March 2008, the 2008 card is used from April 2008 until March 2009, and so on.

25. The card is organized into nine or ten categories of hands. The player should examine her tiles to select one or more target hands from among the various hands or categories of hands listed on the current card.

26. Each hand is marked with its value and a letter "X" or "C." "X" stands for "exposed," meaning that portions of the hand may be exposed through melding prior to the declaration of mah-jongg. "C" stands for "concealed," meaning that no portion of the hand may be revealed to the other players until it is complete.

27. Hands are designated as making up various numbers of tiles gathered into sets. The types of sets are single tiles (which may not be replaced with a joker), pairs (2 identical tiles without jokers), pungs (3 identical tiles, optionally including up to three jokers), kongs (4 identical tiles, optionally including up to four jokers), quints (5 identical tiles, usually necessitating the inclusion of jokers, five being the maximum), sextets (6 identical tiles, see previous note). If the hand includes larger sets, those are called septettes (7 identical tiles), octettes (8 identical tiles), and ninefolds (9 identical tiles).

28. Hands may be marked using one, two, or three colors. The colors symbolize different suits, without being specific as to any one particular suit.

   a. Flowers and winds and "zero" are not associated with any suit, and are always marked in blue.

   b. When a hand is marked using only one color, disregarding winds and flowers and zeroes, and includes numbers from 1 to 9, the hand must be made with tiles of only one suit (any one suit).

   c. When a hand is marked using two colors, disregarding winds and flowers and zeroes, the hand must be made with two suits (any two suits).

   d. When a hand is marked using three colors, disregarding winds and flowers and zeroes, the hand must be made using all three suits (in any combination).

29. When a hand is shown with two sets of tiles in one color, both sets must belong to the same suit (any suit).

30. Hands may be marked with numbers and/or letters. In the absence of parenthetical words saying otherwise, the numbers and/or letters represent specific tiles (as logical per standard usage). When parenthetical words so indicate, the numbers and/or letters may be representative or symbolic of nonspecific tiles, as indicated in parentheses.

31. Parentheticals, if used, always trump the color-coding, if the parenthetical and color-coding appear not to be in perfect accord with one another. That's why parentheticals are included— to clarify something that cannot be clearly symbolized by the color-coding.

32. When used in parentheses, the word "any" always means "any." *Always.* The color-coding used to symbolize the hand may be trumped by the words in parentheses, if present.

33. The phrase "Any 3 Suits," if present, means that the hand must be made using three suits, but the tiles belonging to those suits are not limited to being of any particular suit (it means only that the color-coding is symbolic and representative, without dictating a particular suit).

34. When used in parentheses, the word "only" does not mean "without jokers." For example, if a parenthetical says "Kong Red Dragon Only," that means that no other dragon except red may be used. In such a case, the parenthetical is there only in case a player might think that some other tile might be used.

35. The word "like" means "same" or "alike." The card may show "11 111 1111" in three colors and say "Any Like Nos." This means that the number needn't necessarily be ones, but the number used must be the same number in each of the three suits.

36. Dragons are associated with suits.
    a. Red Dragon is associated with Craks.
    b. Green Dragon is associated with Bams.
    c. White Dragon is associated with Dots.
    d. The term "matching dragon" means that the indicated dragon must be the dragon associated with the suit being used.
    e. "Opposite dragon" means that the dragon must be associated with a suit not being used.

37. Zeroes on the card represent White Dragon. When used as zero, the dragon is no longer associated with a particular suit (it is "suitless"). When "2007" or "2008" is shown on the card, the 2 and the 7 (or the 2 and the 8) must be in the same suit (any suit) and the zeroes must be White Dragon tiles.

38. The card may display dissimilar numbers or letters grouped together in close proximity. Such a close grouping, done purely for aesthetic purposes, does not necessarily constitute a pair, a pung, or a kong. "2007" is not a kong; "NEWS" is not a kong; "13" is not a pair. These terms (kong, pair, etc.) are already clearly defined herein.

THE CHARLESTON

39. Having organized her tiles and selected one or more hands or categories of hands, the player joins the others in entering a phase called the "Charleston" (so called in honor of a dance that was popular during the 1920s, when the game of mah-jongg first became popular). The mah-jongg Charleston comprises two dances consisting of three passes each, the first (right, across,

left) being mandatory, and the second (left, across, right) being optional, followed by an optional "courtesy pass" across the table with the opposite player.

a. In the first Charleston dance, each player shall pass 3 tiles to the player at her right. The tiles must be placed at the corner of the table (outside the area bounded by the four player walls). After relinquishing 3 tiles to her rightmost player, the player may then pick up the 3 tiles passed to her by her left-most player and put them among the tiles of her hand.

b. Each player shall then pass 3 tiles to the player seated opposite. The tiles must be placed within the area bounded by the four player walls, near the center of the opposite player's rack. After relinquishing 3 tiles to her opposite player, the player may then pick up the 3 tiles passed to her by her opposite player and put them among her tiles.

c. For the third step of the first Charleston dance, each player has the option of passing fewer than 3 tiles, by means of a move called the "blind pass." The player to the left of each player must receive 3 tiles, but the player passing tiles is permitted to forward (without looking) up to 3 tiles being passed to her by the player at her right.

    i. In the rare circumstance that no player at the table can comfortably pass as many as 3 tiles, any player may begin. A player may pass 1 or 2 tiles with a promise to pass the remainder shortly. In this manner, as long as at least one player has at least 1 tile to pass, the third movement of the first Charleston dance can be completed.

    ii. When passing left, the player should place the 3 tiles at the corner at her left (outside the area bounded by the four player walls). After relinquishing her 3 tiles, she may pick up the 3 tiles at her right, placed there by the player at her right for her to take.

40. After the "first left" pass (the third movement of the first Charleston dance) has been completed, and before the "second left" pass (the first movement of the second Charleston dance), any player may decree an end to the Charleston, provided that no

player has yet picked up the second 3 tile pass from the player at her right.

   a. No reason or explanation is necessary when stopping the Charleston. (It is unwise to offer a reason or explanation. It's expected that other players will be unhappy when the Charleston is stopped. If asked to provide an explanation, I recommend that the player refuse to give one.)

41. If no player elects to stop the Charleston after the first left, the second Charleston may not be stopped until completed.

   a. When passing the second set of 3 tiles to the left (to commence the first movement of the second Charleston dance), the player shall form the 3 tiles into a small pyramid shape, 1 tile atop a 2-tile base, and place them in the corner of the table at her left (outside the area bounded by the four player walls). This is the only time a pass is to be shaped into a pyramid. After relinquishing the 3 tiles, she may pick up the tiles passed to her by the player at her right.

   b. Each player shall then pass 3 tiles to the player seated opposite. The tiles must be placed within the area bounded by the four player walls, near the center of the opposite player's rack. After relinquishing 3 tiles to her opposite player, the player may then pick up the 3 tiles passed to her by her opposite player.

   c. Each player shall then pass 3 tiles to the right. In this movement, each player has the option of passing fewer than 3 tiles, by means of a blind pass as previously described. The player to the right of each player must receive 3 tiles, but the player passing tiles is permitted to forward (without looking) up to 3 tiles being passed to her by the player at her left.

      i. In the rare circumstance that no player at the table can comfortably pass as many as 3 tiles, any player may begin. A player may pass 1 or 2 tiles with a promise to pass the remainder shortly. In this manner, as long as at least one player has at least 1 tile to pass, the third movement of the second Charleston dance can be completed.

42. Upon the completion of the second Charleston dance (or, if stopped after the first Charleston, upon the announcement that the Charleston is being stopped), an optional "courtesy pass" takes place.

    a. Each player announces to her opposite how many tiles, up to 3, she wishes to exchange.

    b. No player is obliged to exchange more tiles than she desires, thus the player offering the lower number is the one who sets the number of tiles to be exchanged.

43. Once a player has passed to her opposite player the agreed number of tiles and relinquishes them, she may pick up the tiles passed to her and put them among the tiles of her hand. The Charleston phase is now complete.

PLAY

44. After the Charleston, the dealer, provided she is unable to declare mah-jongg, begins the game by discarding a tile.

45. When discarding, the player must speak the name of the tile.

    a. When naming a suit tile, it is customary and proper to say first the number of the tile and then the suit (two words, singular and without the word "of," for example "One Dot" or "One Bam" or "One Crak").

    b. When naming an honor tile, it is customary and proper to say the tile's name in one syllable, omitting the word "wind" or the word "dragon" (for example, "North," "East," "Red," or "Green").

    c. When naming a flower tile, it is customary and proper to say only "Flower" (one should not speak any numbers or words indicated by the images or writing on the flower tile).

    d. As for what to say when discarding a joker tile, see "Jokers" (page 57).

46. Normally, each player in turn, counterclockwise from the dealer, picks a tile from the wall (the same end of the wall used during the deal), bringing her tile total to 14, then discards a tile, returning her hand's tile total to 13.

47. An alternate way to acquire one's 14th tile is by taking a discard.

48. The "window of opportunity" rule. The most recently discarded tile (and *only* the most recently discarded tile) is available for another player to call up until the moment that the next player racks her picked tile or discards.

49. Before picking a tile from the wall, a player should pause a beat in case anyone else wishes to call for the current discard. The pause is beneficial for the game in that it reduces the opportunities for discord. A good rule of thumb is to wait until the previous player has withdrawn her hand from the center of the table before reaching for the end of the wall to pick.

50. Once the tile has been lifted from the wall, the player may not change her mind and put it back on the wall.

51. Picking the tile, she should bring the wall behind her rack and examine it or rack it (place it among the tiles of her racked hand). Her looking at the picked tile does not close the window of opportunity for another to claim the current live discard; racking does close it.

52. Once the tile is lifted from the wall, the player now has 14 tiles in the hand. Having examined her picked tile, whether or not she has racked it, and provided that she cannot claim mah-jongg, she must discard a tile. In the absence of having racked the picked tile, discarding a new tile closes the window of opportunity for another player to claim the previous discard.

53. A discarded tile is "down" and may not be retracted by the discarder once it has been fully named or touched to the tabletop, whichever occurs first.

54. If a player misnames the tile she discarded, she is required to speak the correct name of the tile that was discarded. She is not permitted to retract the tile, once it is down, as defined above. Certain errors may arise from the misnaming of a tile; see "Errors and Penalties" (page 59).

55. Once a discarded tile has been named and placed on the tabletop, it is available for claiming ("calling") by another player (the window of opportunity on that tile is now open).

56. When a tile is discarded, it "covers" all previous discards. Only the current discard may be called. All covered discards are considered dead.

57. When 2 identical tiles are discarded in succession and a player calls, it is the second tile that must be taken.

CLAIMING A DISCARD FOR A MELDED SET

58. Any player may claim the current live discard to make an exposure, provided that certain prerequisites are met:

   a. The player must have enough other identical tiles (jokers are regarded as being "identical" to any nonjoker tile) to form a complete set of the amount of tiles as appropriate for the hand(s) being targeted;

   b. The size of the set being completed must be at minimum 3 identical tiles;

   c. The set completed by the discarded tile must be exposed to the view of the other players.

59. To claim a discard, the player must vocalize the claim.

   a. The player may say anything that clearly and unambiguously lets the other players know that she is claiming the discard. Unlike all other forms of mah-jongg, the player should not say "Pung" or "Kong"; rather, she may say simply "I want that" or "Call" or "Take," for instance.

   b. The player must speak the claim loudly and clearly enough that all players can hear the claim.

   c. The player must speak the claim while the window of opportunity is open (before the next player racks or discards).

60. After vocalizing the claim for the discard, the player should take the discard and put it atop her rack (on the flat area intended for displaying melded sets), and take the other tiles (those that complete the set) from her hand and put them beside the taken discard.

   a. It is permissible to first expose the tiles from the hand, then complete it with the taken discard (rather than first taking, then exposing). The order of the two steps is unimportant.

   b. It is forbidden to take the discard and put it among her tiles resting on the sloping front of her rack, prior to exposing the completed set. See "Errors and Penalties" (page 59).

c. Once the player has exposed tiles from her hand, she is committed to taking the discard. Merely taking the discard and putting it atop the rack (without exposing tiles from the hand) is a reversible action. See "Changes of Heart" (page 64).

d. When the meld contains jokers, it's best to "sandwich" jokers between natural tiles, making it easier for other players to tell where one meld ends and another begins.

e. It's customary to put the first meld at the left end of the rack. Subsequent melds are lined up to the right, in chronological order (the order they are exposed).

f. The player is permitted to change the size of her exposure (adding or subtracting tiles) up to the time that she discards. Since she is committed to making an exposure, the minimum number of tiles that may be left atop the rack is 3.

61. After a player has melded a set, she must discard a tile.

62. After a player has melded a set and discarded, the order of play continues from she who melded (not from she who discarded).

TWO PLAYERS CLAIM SAME DISCARD

63. When two players claim the same discarded tile, the tile doesn't necessarily go to the player who spoke first. Provided that both claims (i) are spoken within a reasonably short time, and (ii) the second claim is spoken before the first speaker has exposed tiles from her hand, conflicting claims are resolved as follows:

a. When two players claim a discarded tile for exposure, the player nearest in turn to the discarder gets the tile.

b. When two players claim a discarded tile, one for exposure and one for mah-jongg, the mah-jongg call trumps the exposure call.

c. When two players claim a discarded tile for mah-jongg, the player nearest in turn to the discarder gets the tile.

CLAIMING A DISCARD FOR A WIN

64. Any player may claim the current live discard for mah-jongg at any time, (i) regardless of whose turn it is, and (ii) regardless of the size of the set completed by the discard.

65. To claim a discard for mah-jongg, the player must vocalize the claim.

    a. The player may say anything that clearly and unambiguously lets the other player know that she is claiming the tile for a win. The rules do not specify what must be said; she may say "Mah-jongg," "Maj," or "That's it," for instance.

    b. The player must speak the claim loudly and clearly enough that all players can hear the claim.

    c. The player must speak the claim while the window of opportunity is open (before the player whose turn follows the discarder's racks or discards).

66. After speaking the claim for mah-jongg, the player must expose all her tiles and take the discard to complete the hand.

    a. It is permissible to first take the discard and put it atop her rack, then expose tiles from the hand (the order of the two steps is unimportant).

    b. It is forbidden to take the discard and put it in the hand, among the tiles on the sloping front of her rack, prior to exposing the hand, subject to the penalty of "death." See "Errors & Penalties" (page 59).

    c. The hand must be displayed as sets, organized in the order shown on the card. It's customary for the hand to be arrayed in accord with the point of view of the winner.

    d. The winner is required to identify the winning hand to the satisfaction of the other players.

67. The winner is required to inform all other players how much each player must pay. No other player should assist the winner in doing this. It is likely that the player will have to repeat the score, due to the fact that the nonwinners are probably kvetching instead of listening.

WINNING BY SELF-PICK

68. A player who picks a tile that completes her hand must announce the fact aloud to the other players.

    a. The rules do not specify what the player must say upon making mah-jongg. It's permissible to say "I picked it," or "Mah-jongg," or "Maj"; she may say anything that conveys the news to the others.

    b. It's best to say "I picked it," because this has ramifications as to the amount won, not that the players will notice or remember (due to the likelihood that they will begin kvetching immediately upon hearing the maj declaration).

69. The winner must then display the hand.

    a. The hand must be displayed as separate sets, organized in the order shown on the card. It's customary for the hand to be arrayed in accord with the point of view of the winner.

    b. The winner is required to identify the winning hand to the satisfaction of the other players.

70. The winner is required to inform all other players how much each player must pay. No other player should assist the winner in doing this. It is likely that the winner will have to repeat the score and how it was calculated, since the other players will have been telling their own tales of woe to one another rather than paying attention the first time she so announced.

SCORING & PAYMENT

71. The value of a hand is shown on the card, to the right of that hand.

72. There are only two ways that a hand can be won: by discard or by self-pick.

    a. When a hand is won by discard, nondiscarders pay single value, and discarder pays double the value of the hand.

    b. When a hand is won by self-pick, all nonwinners pay double the value of the hand.

73. When a hand is made without any jokers, and provided that the hand is not listed in the "Singles And Pairs" section of the card

(which cannot contain jokers anyway), all nonwinners pay the winner double the value they would otherwise pay.

   a. A hand is considered jokerless if no jokers are present in the hand at the time that the player declares mah-jongg, regardless of whether or not the hand had previously contained jokers.

74. It's possible for a score to be doubled more than once; it's simple math to double a number and then double it again. As of this writing, the lowest-value hand on the card is 25. Given the above, the most that could be paid by one nonwinner for a lowest-value hand would be 100 (double for discarder or double for self-pick, and double again for jokerless).

75. Payment may be made in chips or in coins, or score may be kept on paper.

   a. When payment is made in chips, the value of the chips must be determined and agreed before commencement of play.

   b. When payment is made in coins, one point customarily equals one U.S. cent (one hundredth of one U.S. dollar).

   c. When keeping score on paper, award positive points to winners and negative points to nonwinners, per the above.

76. When playing with coins:

   a. You are on your own. Playing for money is against the law in some parts of the United States. The police are not likely to bust a bunch of ladies playing merely for quarters and dimes (especially when small change is exchanged between players only and the house is not taking a rake), but be aware of the law, and be discreet. If you are caught gambling, this author will disavow any knowledge of your actions.

   b. Many players play for a maximum purse, called a "pie." Each player at the table brings the same purse to a game session. Some tables play for a $3 maximum, some for a $5 maximum, and some for a $10 maximum. When a player has emptied her purse and when playing with a "pie" table rule, she plays for free until she wins again. Then she is subject to payments like anyone else until she "goes pie" again, and so on.

GAME OVER

77. After a player has collected payment from the nonwinners, a new game may be played.

78. If the wall is completely depleted without anyone winning, a "wall game" is declared. No player has won. A new game is played.
   a. All tiles are thrown in;
   b. The tiles are turned facedown;
   c. The tiles are shuffled;
   d. Walls are built;
   e. The player to the right of the previous dealer rolls the dice to commence the new game.

79. Each hand is a "game" unto itself; the players may disband after any hand. It's customary to have a predetermined hour when play will cease, or a player may announce that she wishes to depart after one more hand. Each hand lasts approximately fifteen minutes. It's polite to give notice of one's wish to depart or disband "after this next hand."

JOKERS

80. Jokers are wild. They may be used to represent any other tile.

81. Jokers may only be used in sets of identical tiles consisting of 3 or more tiles (pungs, kongs, quints, sextets, etc.).
   a. Given the foregoing, it should not be necessary to add that jokers may *never* be used in a pair or to represent a single tile.
   b. Given the frequency with which the question is asked, it was deemed necessary to add the previous sentence anyway.

82. When taking a discard for exposure, the player may fill the exposure with as many jokers as she wishes. There is no requirement that the player must have any minimum number of natural tiles in the exposure.

83. When using jokers to build a set concealed in the hand, the player may fill the set with as many jokers as she wishes. There is no requirement that the player must have any minimum number of natural tiles to complete a set.

84. Jokers may *never* be passed during the Charleston (including the courtesy pass). A player who receives a joker during the Charleston and does not return it to the passer is as guilty of breaking the rules as is the one who passed it. A player who receives a joker in the Charleston must return it and request a legal tile.

85. The only ways that a player may obtain a joker are as follows:
    a. From the wall (either during the deal, or by self-pick), or:
    b. By redeeming it from someone's exposure, using a natural tile matching the tiles in the exposure.

86. The rules governing redemption of jokers are as follows:
    a. A player may only redeem a joker on her own turn, while there are 14 tiles in her hand (including any melds). For the sake of clarity, this means that she must first either pick a tile from the wall, or claim a discard and make a legal exposure, before she may redeem a joker.
    b. To redeem the joker, the player must be holding a natural tile that matches the nonjoker(s) among the exposed set.
    c. The player may redeem a joker from any exposure on any rack, including her own.
    d. When redeeming the joker from another player's rack, the player may either make the exchange by herself, or with the assistance of the player to whom the joker belonged.
    e. The player is permitted to redeem multiple jokers, from multiple racks, on a single play.
    f. When redeeming a joker, it is *not* necessary to expose a set. The joker may be placed within the hand and used in any way the player wishes at any time subsequent to the redemption of it.
    g. It is *not* permissible to put a joker on any player's rack and take a natural tile. Redemption is a one-way street; "reverse redemption" is not allowed.

87. Jokers atop a dead player's rack are redeemable, assuming that the dead player has previously reracked any illegal melds. See "Death Penalty" (page 63).

88. When redemption of a joker directly results in mah-jongg, it is

deemed a win by self-pick. (If the player is already holding a re-deemable tile and takes a discard for exposure, followed imme-diately by redeeming the joker for a win, the win is deemed to be by self-pick.)

89. It is permissible to discard a joker, usually done either because the player is targeting a Singles And Pairs hand or because the player needs a safe discard. The rules governing the discarding of jokers are as follows:

    a. When the dealer's first discard is a joker, she should say its name: "Joker."

    b. Subsequently discarded jokers may be named same as the most recent discard. The player may say "Same" or she may repeat the name of the most recent discard. This is done so that other players pay attention to what is discarded with their eyes as well as their ears.

    c. When a joker has been discarded, it covers *all* previous dis-cards (including the named "same" discard). The joker itself, and *all* previous discards, are *all* considered dead tiles, and *nothing* may be taken by any player. (In the foregoing sen-tence, italics have been used to indicate emphasis. Please read this rule two or three times until it is clearly under-stood.)

ERRORS & PENALTIES

90. Errors in the deal.

    a. If a player rolls the dice and breaks the wall out of turn, the game is played anyway. The dice revert to the player who was supposed to deal that game, and the next time the dice come to the player who dealt out of turn, her deal is skipped.

    b. If a player doesn't get her 4 tiles (or her 1 tile) at the proper moment during the deal, other players should do their best to replace their stacks in reverse order taken.

    c. If the wrong wall is used during the deal, players should try to undo the error if possible. If the error is discovered after the deal has been completed and can't be remedied, the walls should be rearranged in any manner deemed satisfactory, so as to prevent further errors.

d. If any error is discovered during the dealing process, it should be remedied immediately if possible. If the misdeal cannot be reasonably and satisfactorily remedied, all tiles should be returned to the center of the table, the walls should be broken, the tiles should be reshuffled, the walls should be rebuilt, and the dice should be rerolled by the same dealer.

e. Although it is customary to wait until all players have received all their tiles before looking at them, the official rules do not provide a penalty for racking during the deal.

91. Error in the Charleston. If a player takes a pass out of order, she should put those tiles back and take the correct pass. If the error cannot be remedied, the game is restarted; all tiles are thrown in and reshuffled, and the walls are rebuilt. Same dealer rolls again.

92. Wrong tile count.

a. If a player has the wrong number of tiles in her hand before the Charleston begins, a misdeal is declared; all tiles are thrown in and reshuffled, and the walls are rebuilt. Same dealer rolls again.

b. If the player at East's left is short 1 tile during or after the Charleston, and dealer has not yet made her first discard, this player (and only this player) may take the tile from the end of the wall to right her hand.

c. If a player has the wrong number of tiles in her hand at any time after the dealer has made her first discard, her hand is dead. See "Death Penalty" (page 63).

d. If two players have the wrong number of tiles in their hands at any time after the dealer has discarded, both are dead; the survivors continue playing.

e. If three players have the wrong number of tiles in their hands at any time after the dealer has discarded, the game is played over. Same dealer rolls again.

93. No picking ahead. It is forbidden to pick the tile from the wall

before the player at your left has discarded her tile and spoken its name. In a home game, a player who picks ahead once should be warned, politely but firmly. A player who picks ahead a second time, or who picks ahead in a tournament, is subject to the death penalty. See "Death Penalty" (page 63). *(Note: at one time, a very long time ago, picking ahead was allowed. Some elderly players still use and teach the practice. Use of outlawed practices such as this one fall under the category of "table rules," and are not defined herein.)*

94. No peeking at the blind pass. In a tournament, a player who peeks at tiles she is blind passing during the Charleston is subject to the death penalty. In a home game, a first-time offender should be warned, politely but firmly.

95. Misnaming a discard. The penalty varies depending on the circumstances and repercussions of the error, as follows:

  a. If the player corrects the error and correctly names the tile that was discarded, without having caused any cascading errors, no penalty applies. Having been named correctly, the tile may be called for exposure.

  b. If another player calls the misnamed tile for exposure, the tile cannot be taken (since it does not match the set the caller is making), and no penalty applies. Having been named correctly, the tile may be called for exposure.

  c. If another player calls the misnamed tile for mah-jongg, the game ceases. The player who misnamed the tile pays the caller four times the value of the hand held by the caller. No other player has to pay the caller.

96. Putting a taken discard into the hand prior to exposure of a set or the hand. In a home game, whether or not to penalize such an act is at the discretion of the players. In a tournament, it may be punishable by the death penalty (at the discretion of the tournament judge).

97. Exposure in error.

  a. A player who calls a tile for exposure, then changes her mind, may do so without penalty, provided that the caller did not expose tiles from her hand.

b. A player who exposes an illegal set (for instance, exposing a set containing mismatched tiles) is subject to the death penalty if she does not or cannot remedy the exposure before discarding. The only legal sets are pungs and higher, and all tiles in the set must be identical (jokers count as being "identical" to any natural tiles in the set).

c. A player who exposes a set that clearly indicates an illegal hand (for instance, exposing a type of set only possible in a concealed hand, or a second set that cannot legally coexist with a previously exposed set) has a dead hand.

98. Mah-jongg in error.

a. If a player declares mah-jongg but immediately withdraws the declaration without exposing her hand, and without causing any other player to expose or destroy a hand or the wall, no penalty is incurred and the game may continue.

b. If a player declares mah-jongg and exposes her hand, and it is subsequently determined that her hand is invalid, she is dead. The other players may continue playing as before, provided that:

   i. No other player had exposed her own hand;
   ii. No other player had destroyed her own hand;
   iii. No other player had destroyed the wall;
   iv. No other player had tried to claim the same tile, either for exposure or for mah-jongg.

c. If a player exposes or destroys her own hand after another player has declared mah-jongg in error, she too is dead.

d. If two players expose or destroy their hands after another player has declared mah-jongg in error, the game ceases. The player who initiated the cascade by erroneously declaring pays double the value of her own hand to the sole surviving player; the other two players pay and receive nothing.

e. If a player destroys the wall after another player has declared mah-jongg in error, the game ceases. She must pay the two surviving players the lowest hand value on the card.

f. When a player declares mah-jongg in error on a discard, the discard remains in the dead hand unless another player had claimed the tile for mah-jongg; the other claimant may have the tile once the error has been acknowledged. (The discard may not be taken merely to complete a set for exposure; it remains in the dead hand.)

99. Unwise discard, resulting in a win by an opponent. The official rules do not penalize unwise discarding, but in tournaments, under certain circumstances, it is a punishable act. (*Home game use of penalties for, or prohibitions against, unwise discarding fall under the category of "table rules," and are not defined herein.*)

100. If a player plays out of turn and discards another player's winning tile, discarder pays four times the value of the winner's hand (other players do not pay).

DEATH PENALTY

101. A player may be declared dead for several reasons, as follows:
   a. Holding a hand with too few or too many tiles after the dealer's first discard.
   b. Showing exposures that clearly do not match a hand on the current card.
   c. Showing exposures that clearly indicate a hand that cannot be completed (as can be seen by discards or by other players' exposures).
   d. Showing exposures that clearly indicate a hand that is supposed to be concealed.
   e. Showing an exposure of mismatched tiles.
   f. Picking ahead or playing out of turn.
   g. Peeking at the blind pass.

102. To declare a player dead, a player may at any time issue a death challenge. The challenge should be spoken declaratively. The customary expression of the declaration is, "I'm sorry, but you're dead."
   a. *Asking* a player "Are you dead?" is the same thing as declaring a player dead. Whether expressing the death challenge

as a declaration or a question, the same result occurs. All eyes turn to the challenged player's rack.

b. Even making quizzical noises or meaningful suggestive gestures or looks could constitute a death challenge.

c. Accordingly, if you are unsure if you want to issue a death challenge, best to remain completely silent, still, and expressionless.

103. After a death challenge, the challenged player has two possible choices of action:

a. She may accede, acknowledging that her hand is dead, and stop playing;

b. She may deny that her hand is dead, and continue playing. No explanation need be provided (she is not required to explain to the challenger what hand she is making).

104. If a challenged player denies that her hand is dead, she continues playing. Once the hand is ended, she must reveal her hand to the scrutiny of all, so that it can be determined whether the death challenge had been in error or not.

a. If it is determined that the challenged player's hand had indeed been dead, the challenged player pays the challenger the value of the lowest-scoring hand on the card.

b. If it is determined that the challenged player's hand had been valid all along, the challenger pays the challenged player the value of the lowest-scoring hand on the card.

105. A player who realizes that her own hand is dead should not call herself dead; she should continue playing defensively until called dead or until the game ends.

106. When a player is declared dead, any illegal exposures she'd made just prior to the death declaration (such exposures having clearly shown that her hand was dead) must be returned to the sloping front of her rack.

107. When a dead player, after returning her illegal exposures to the sloping front of her rack, still has jokers among her remaining exposures, those jokers are still considered "alive"; they are still available for redemption.

108. A player whose hand had been declared dead does not pick or

discard, and may not comment on any other player's hand. At the conclusion of the game, the dead player pays the winner the same as any other nonwinner.

CHANGES OF HEART

109. Discarding a tile. Up until the time a player has completely named her discard or touched it to the table, she may change her mind about discarding it.

110. Picking from the wall. Up until the time a player has lifted the tile from the wall, she may change her mind about taking it.

111. Taking a discard. Up until the time a player has exposed tiles from her hand, she may change her mind about taking it.

112. Declaring mah-jongg. Provided that no other player has exposed or destroyed a hand or the wall, and provided that the declarer has not exposed her hand, she may change her mind.

113. Amount of tiles in an exposed set. Provided that the player has not yet discarded, she may change the amount of tiles in the set she has exposed (but she has committed to melding and may not take them all back).

114. Passing tiles in the Charleston. Provided that the other player has not yet picked up the pass, she may change the tiles she is passing. (It is bad etiquette to take them back if the other player is reaching to take them.)

SEAT ROTATION

115. When playing with four players, in order to mix things up and let players sit in different seats, it's recommended that players rotate seats every so often.

116. The original dealer ("first East") is designated "pivot." Every second time the dice come to the pivot, she exchanges seats with the player at her right.

117. The official rules say that the dice should remain with the seat (and not move with the pivot), but a mathematical analysis shows that each player gets an equal number of deals if the

dice go with the pivot when she moves one seat to the right. This author recommends that the pivot ("first East") always be the first to deal after a seat rotation (this being the *only* departure from the official NMJL rules recommended by this author).

FIVE OR MORE PLAYERS

118. When five players are present, there are two ways all players may be accommodated:

   a. The fifth player may rotate into the play, four players playing at a time and a different one sitting out each game;

   b. The rotating fifth player may act as "bettor," betting on which player will win the game she is sitting out.

119. At the beginning of the game, dice are rolled to determine which player will sit out. Low roller sits out. In case of a tie, the low rollers roll again until the tie is broken.

120. After each game, the player who dealt the just-completed hand shall relinquish her seat to the fifth player.

121. When the fifth player is acting as bettor, she shall silently examine each player's tiles after the completion of the Charleston and before the dealer makes her first discard, and silently make a record of her bet.

122. The bet may be in writing, on a pad of paper, or it may be recorded using the plastic disc called a "bettor" (and also known as a "wind indicator"), if such a device is present with the mahjongg set being used.

123. Bettor may bet on any player at the table, or she may bet on a wall game.

124. The bettor must not reveal her bet to the players until after the hand has been played out.

125. The bettor is not permitted to change her bet once play has commenced.

126. The bettor is not permitted to make any comment on the players' hands or on the game until the game has been completed and nonwinners have paid the winner; failure to comply with this rule causes her bet to be invalidated.

127. Once the game is completed, bettor reveals her bet. She pays or receives same as the "bet-on" player, including penalties, if any.

128. When bettor predicted a wall game and a wall game occurs, each player pays the bettor the value of the lowest-scoring hand on the card.

129. When six players are present, two may sit out while four play. After the first game has been played, the two may roll dice to determine which shall be seated first. It's not necessary to roll again thereafter; players rotate back to the table in the order they rotate out.

130. The two may act as bettors, recording bets on two separate sheets of paper. They may not discuss their bets with each other.

THREE OR FEWER PLAYERS

131. When three players are present, four walls are built. Tiles are dealt only to the three players. There is no Charleston; game begins with dealer discarding a tile.

132. When two players are present, four walls are built. The two players sit opposite each other. Tiles are dealt only to the two players. There is no Charleston; game begins with dealer discarding a tile.

B. How to Play American Mah-Jongg

Mah-Jongg is played similarly to card games of the rummy family. The goal is to form a complete mah-jongg hand. Players take turns counterclockwise around the table. Each player, on her turn, takes a tile into the hand, then discards a tile. Most of the time, then, the player is holding 13 tiles, but brings a 14th tile into the hand every time it's her turn. The goal in mah-jongg is to form a complete 14-tile hand. And to do it before anyone else does. At the point when the player's 14 tiles form a valid mah-jongg hand, the player declares mah-jongg, and the other players pay her according to the value of the hand as listed on the card.

The National Mah Jongg League issues a new card every year on April 1. The card is a list of hands that may be played during the current year. All the players must be playing from the current yearly NMJL card. Contact information for the league is given in Appendix 2.

BUILDING THE WALL & DEALING

To begin, the players shuffle the 152 tiles (the basic Chinese 144-tile set plus 8 jokers) and build them into a square wall, two tiles high. Each player's wall is nineteen stacks long, lined up behind her rack.

The dealer rolls dice to determine where to break the wall. Let's say the dealer rolls a 9. This tells her that the wall is to be broken after the ninth stack from the right side of her wall.

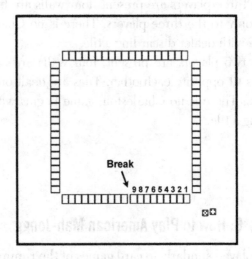

Having made the break, the dealer removes the dice from the center of the table and places them to her right (the next dealer will find the dice handily placed at her left).

The tiles to the right of the break remain where they are. This is the back end of the wall. The deal commences with the tiles to the left of the break (clockwise from the break).

Dealer rolls dice.

Dealer breaks wall.

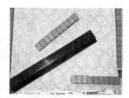

Dealer serves wall.

Dealer takes two stacks.

Player at right takes.

Dealer's opposite takes.

The dealer herself takes the first two stacks (4 tiles) to the left of the break. Then, the player at the dealer's right takes the next two stacks (4 tiles). The player across from the dealer takes the next two stacks. The player at the dealer's left takes the next two stacks.

This continues, with each player taking two stacks in turn, until all players have taken two stacks three times. Each player now has 12 tiles.

Left player takes.

Dealer takes two more stacks.

Left player serves wall.

Right player takes.

Opposite player takes.

Left player takes.

Dealer takes again.   *Right player takes.*   *Opposite takes.*

Note that although players are taking turns counterclockwise, the tiles are removed from the wall in a clockwise direction.

To finish up the deal, the dealer takes 2 more tiles, and the other players all take 1. The dealer takes the top tiles from the first and third stacks. Then the player to the dealer's right takes the end tile. Then the player across from the dealer takes the top tile from the end stack. Then the player at the dealer's left takes the end tile.

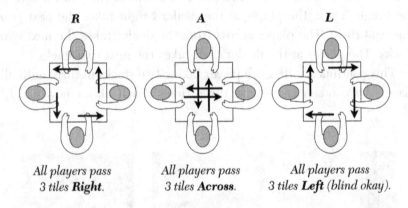

| R | A | L |

All players pass   *All players pass*   *All players pass*
*3 tiles **Right**.*   *3 tiles **Across**.*   *3 tiles **Left** (blind okay).*

Now the dealer is holding 14 tiles, and all the other players hold 13 tiles. Each player places her tiles on the sloping front of her rack, arranging the tiles in the hand to begin playing.

Left player takes.   *Dealer takes*   *Right player takes*
                            "1 and 3."   *end tile.*

*Opposite takes
top tile.*

*Left player takes
end tile.*

*Players rack
and arrange.*

ASSESSING THE HAND

Each player examines her tiles to determine which patterns on the card she can shoot for. It often happens that the initial mess does not clearly suggest one particular hand. Experienced players see numerous possibilities, and may keep multiple possible hands open as the tiles shape the hand.

If a hand contains a fairly large number of wind tiles, the player would be well advised to go for a Winds-Dragons hand. If a hand contains a fairly large proportion of odd-numbered suit tiles, the player might want to target a 13579 hand. The most common type of hand is a Consecutive Run hand, made of sequentially numbered sets of suit tiles.

Let's look at the card now . . .

THE CARD

In the American game, a hand doesn't qualify for mah-jongg unless it matches one of the hands listed on the card. The card is issued by the National Mah Jongg League in New York City, and the card changes on April 1 of every year. Changing the card keeps the game fresh and challenging for its devoted players. It also makes it a challenge to be specific (and timely) in a book like this one.

The card is a list of hands, categorized into specific types of patterns. Some of the pattern types remain constant from year to year, and some of the pattern types change to keep the game new.

The card is folded twice. Unfolded, it can rest on the table in front of the player's rack for easy reference.

The back of the card (the outside when folded) lists the major rules of the game. The "meat" of the card is the front of the card (the inside when folded). The two folds of the card divide it into three panes. Each pane has three or more sections, listing hands in categories or "families."

Left Pane

- **This Year:** Each hand in this section contains tiles that represent the year that the card was issued. For instance, the hands in the upper-left section of the 2007 card all require the inclusion of a 2 and 7 of the same suit, together with a pair of white dragons.
- **2468:** Each hand in the middle section of the left pane requires even-numbered suit tiles (and sometimes flowers and dragons).
- **Change-Up:** The bottom-left section of the card is a Change-Up section. The type of hands in this section are different every year. There may even be more than one Change-Up section. The bottom-left section often involves hands that represent simple addition or multiplication.

Middle Pane

- **Quints:** There is at least one quint (a five-of-a-kind grouping) in each hand in this family.
- **Consecutive Run:** This section comprises hands of consecutive numbers.
- **13579:** The hands in this section consist of odd numbers only.

Right Pane

- **Winds-Dragons:** The upper-right family centers on the wind and dragon tiles (the honor tiles).
- **369:** The hands in this section use 3's, 6's, and 9's. And some of the hands use flowers and/or dragon tiles.
- **Singles And Pairs:** At the bottom left of the card is the hardest section of them all, because jokers can't be used here. Every hand is made of pairs and/or single tiles only.

READING THE CARD—GENERAL PRINCIPLES

The colors on the card indicate that different suits must be used. If a hand is shown in all one color on the card, the hand can be made in any one suit. If a hand is shown in two colors (red and green), then you must use two different suits (any two suits) to make the hand. When a hand is shown in three colors, it must be made in all three suits.

Winds and flowers are always shown in blue, even though winds and flowers are suitless. More about the color-coding on page 74 (this is an aspect of reading the card that frequently trips up novices).

The numbers on the card are sometimes flexible. For example, many hands in the Consecutive Run section may be made using any consecutive numbers (not only the numbers shown). When in doubt, see the words in parentheses following the hand. The words in parentheses always trump the specific colors, letters, or numbers used to symbolize the content of the hand.

The letter "D" stands for dragons. The number 0 stands for White Dragon (affectionately referred to as "soap" by American players). But when used as zeroes, soaps are suitless (you are not required to use Dot tiles with zeroes). When the card designers wish to specify a specific dragon, the letters "G" and "R" are used for green and red. Long ago, White Dragon was abbreviated "Wh," and it may happen that a future card may again use that abbreviation.

To the right of the symbolic representation of the hand and a parenthetical descriptor (if any), each hand is marked "X" or "C" and a value is shown. "X" stands for "exposed," meaning the player is permitted to make exposures prior to making mah-jongg. "C" stands for "concealed," meaning the player is not permitted to make exposures prior to making mah-jongg.

The value of the hand comes into play when settling up at the end of the hand, if the player wins on that particular hand. In general, the more difficult a hand is to make, the greater its value. More about hand values in "Scoring and Payment" (page 93).

THE COLOR-CODING—FREQUENTLY MISUNDERSTOOD BY BEGINNERS

The color-coding on the card never dictates which suits must be used (green never means Bams are required; red never means Craks are required; blue never means Dots are required). The colors indicate only how many suits are to be used. When two colors are used, the player may make the hand with any two out of the three possible suits.

The color-coding on the card cannot always convey the complete story of how the hand can be made. When the color-coding isn't sufficient to explain the requirements of a particular hand, the card designer writes a parenthetical to give more information. In such cases, the parenthetical always trumps the color-coding.

For example, perhaps the card displays a quint hand, shown with a quint of a wind tile, a kong of dragons, and quint of a numbered suit tile (shown in a different color from the dragons). Perhaps the parenthetical says "any tile of any suit, kong any dragon."

NNNNN DDDD 11111 (Quint Any Wind & Any No. In Any Suit, Kong Any Dragon) . . . X 40
Blue   Red   Green

Note that although the representation of the hand shows five N's, the parenthetical says "any wind." This means that not only N's, but also E's, W's, or S's may be used (there must be five of the same wind; jokers are needed).

Note that although the representation of the hand shows four red D's, the parenthetical says "any dragon." This means that not only red, but also green or white may be used (they must be four *identical* dragons, not four different dragons; jokers are permitted).

Note that although the representation of the hand shows five green 1's, the parenthetical says "any no. in any suit." This means exactly what it says. The color-coding may be disregarded because the parenthetical trumps the color-coding. The words "any suit" mean just that: *any* suit. The numbered suit tile could be in the same suit as the dragon, or a different suit, regardless of the color-coding, because the parenthetical is the final word on the matter. And of course it could be any number (not only 1's). And of course jokers are needed.

Sometimes there is no parenthetical following the symbolic representation of the hand. In the absence of a parenthetical, the hand must be made as shown (using the exact numbers or letters indicated, and using the exact number of suits indicated by the color-coding).

READING THE CARD—EXAMPLE HANDS

Don't look for the following hands on your current NMJL card. These are only examples to aid you in understanding how the card works.

Example "This Year" Hand

Every year the "This Year" section changes name. In 2006 (when this book was written), this section of the card was called "2006." In 2007, it's called "2007," and so on. The following example might be found in a hypothetical 2007 card.

NEWS 2007 GGG   RRR (Any 2 and 7 Same Suit, Pung Green & Red Dragon Only) . . . X 25
Blue   Blue   Green   Red

A 2007 card might have a hand like the above example. The word "any" in the parenthetical means that the 2 and 7 have to be in the same suit . . . *any* suit. Any one of the following examples would be acceptable to score the above example hand.

(2 and 7 in Craks.)
(2 and 7 in Dots.)
(2 and 7 in Bams.)

NEWS means that the hand must have one each of the wind tiles. These tiles being different from one another, NEWS is four single tiles (it is not a kong). Therefore, the player is not permitted to use jokers for any of these tiles, and the player cannot expose NEWS before the hand is complete. In this hand, jokers may be used only in the pungs of green and red dragons.

Because 2007 is made of two singles and a pair of White Dragons, jokers may not be used in 2007. And 2007 cannot be exposed until the hand is complete.

The red "X" to the right indicates that the player is permitted to call discards for exposure prior to the hand being complete. The 25 indicates the value of the hand when completed.

Although this hand is marked "X" for exposable, since NEWS and 2007 are not exposable groupings, only the dragon pungs can be exposed (and only the dragon pungs can incorporate jokers).

Example 2468 Hand

Every hand in the 2468 family is composed of even-numbered suit tiles. And sometimes flowers and dragons.

22	444	DDDD	666	88	...............................X25
Blue	Blue	Blue	Blue	Blue	

This example hand has no parenthetical, because the hand needs no explanation to those who are familiar with how to read the card. The hand is entirely in one suit; a pair of 2's, a pung of 4's, a kong of dragons, pung of 6's, and pair of 8's. No substitutions permitted.

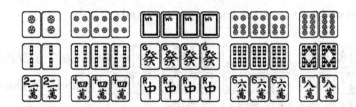

If the hand is made in Dots, the dragons must be white. If made in Bams, the dragons must be green. If made in Craks, the dragons must be red. Because jokers may be used only in pungs or kongs or greater, the two pairs in this hand may not contain any jokers.

In the above example, one joker is used in the pung of 4's; two jokers are used in the kong of dragons; and three jokers are used for the pung of 6's. The pair of 2's and the pair of 8's must both be natural (free of jokers).

Example Change-Up Hand

The lower part of the left pane of the card changes every year. Hands in this section often represent simple mathematical equations. A past favorite is to use groups of numbers that add up to 11.

>   **FFFFFF   333 + 888 = 11 or FFFFFF   333 + 888 = 11........X 30**
>   Blue   Blue   Blue   Blue Blue   Green   Red   Blue

This example shows a hand that can be in either one suit or three suits. It requires a sextet of flowers (six flowers), a pung of 3's and a pung of 8's, and a pair of 1's (11).

The hand is exposable prior to going mah-jongg, and it's worth 30 points (30 cents if playing for coins). Jokers may be used in any set except the pair.

Example Quints Hand

Every hand in the Quints section contains at least one quint (a five-of-a-kind set).

>   **55555   4444   333   22 (These Nos. Only)................X 45**
>   Blue   Blue   Blue   Blue

This example is a one-suit hand, and may only be made with a quint of 5's, a kong of 4's, a pung of 3's, and a pair of 2's. It's exposable, and it's worth 45.

Jokers may be used in all sets except the pair. (The word "only" does not mean "without jokers.") The quint, of course, cannot be made *without* a joker, since there are only four of each tile (except the jokers and the flowers).

Example Consecutive Run Hand

The numbers shown in the Consecutive Runs section are sometimes only symbolic of consecutive numbers. If the card shows a kong of 1's, and the parenthetical says "any consecutive nos.," then the kong can be any number (not only 1's).

111   222   333   444   55 (Any 3 Suits, Any 5 Consecutive Nos.) . . . . X 25
Green Green Red Red Blue

This example hand is shown in three colors. If the card had a hand like this, you could make it with any five sequential numbers. The first two numbers of the sequence must be in one suit. The second two numbers of the sequence must be in a second suit. And the final pair would have to be in the remaining suit. Each of the three following examples would all qualify for this hand.

2's and 3's in one suit, 4's and 5's in a second suit, and 6's in the third suit.

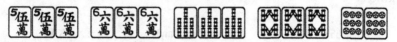

5's and 6's in one suit, 7's and 8's in a second suit, and 9's in the third suit.

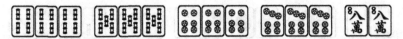

4's and 5's in one suit, 6's and 7's in a second suit, and 8's in the third suit.

Note each example shows five consecutive numbers in three suits. The first two consecutive numbers are in one suit, the next two consecutive numbers are in the second suit, and the final pair is in the remaining suit.

The key to understanding this particular hand is the parenthetical. It says "Any 3 Suits, Any 5 Consecutive Nos." The meaning of the words in the parentheses always trumps whatever you might think the color-coding means. One might think that because the 1's and 2's are green, that the first two groupings of the hand have to be in Bams (the green suit). But not so. One might think that because the 3's and 4's are red, that the second two groupings of the hand have to be in Craks (the red suit). But no. The parenthetical contains the key word "any." And the word "any" always means exactly that: *any*. If the parenthetical says "any 5 consecutive numbers," then the hand can be made with *any* five consecutive numbers. Jokers may of course be used in any of the sets except the pair.

Example 13579 Hand

All hands in the 13579 section are made of odd-numbered suit tiles only. And the occasional set of flowers or dragons.

11	33	11	33	55	1111 (Any 3 Suits, Kong 1, 3, or 5) . . . . C 30
Green	Green	Red	Red	Red	Blue

This is a three-suit hand, since it's shown in three colors on the card. The hand requires five pairs, so it is very difficult to make. The only easy part is the kong—jokers can be used in the kong, and the kong can be any odd number from 1 to 5.

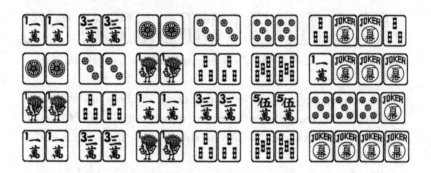

The pairs cannot contain jokers, but the kong may use as many as four.

Example Winds-Dragons Hand

The hands in the upper-right section of the card use the wind and dragon tiles, and sometimes flowers. When suit tiles are used, E and W are considered "even" winds, and N and S are considered "odd" winds.

FF	NNN	SSS	11	11	11 (Pairs Any Like Odd Nos.) . . . . X 35
Blue	Blue	Blue	Green	Blue	Red

If a card had a hand such as the above, it would also have an opposite hand (pungs of E and W, and pairs of any like even numbers).

As always, jokers may not be used in the pairs.

Example 369 Hand

The 369 family uses only 3's, 6's, and 9's, as well as some flowers and dragons.

3333	66	DD	66	9999 (Any 3 Suits) . . . . X 30
Green	Green	Red	Blue	Blue

This example hand requires the player to use a pair of "opposite" dragons. Whatever two suits are used for the 3's, 6's, and 9's, the dragons must be from the remaining suit. Jokers may never be used in pairs.

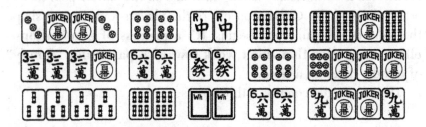

Example Singles And Pairs Hand

The bottom-right corner of the card is the hardest section. Because every hand is composed of single tiles and pairs, jokers are impossible to use, and the player has to pick luckily.

11   22   33   44   55   66   77 (Any Run 7 Pairs) . . . . C 45
Blue Blue Blue Blue Blue Blue Blue

This example hand is one suit only. The pairs must be sequential, and can start with 1's, 2's, or 3's.

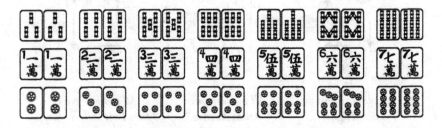

The hands in the Singles And Pairs section often use concepts of other sections of the card. There'll be an odd numbers hand, an even numbers hand, a Consecutive Run hand, a "This Year" hand, and so on.

Now that you know how to read the card, you can choose tiles to pass in the Charleston.

THE CHARLESTON

During the Roaring Twenties, when mah-jongg became all the rage, the most popular dance craze was the Charleston. In mah-jongg, the Charleston is an intricate "dance" in which all the players pass tiles to other players. The Charleston offers the players a chance to shape the hand before game play begins. **It's a process of elimination— eliminating tiles that don't work toward a particular "family" of hands, three at a time.**

The Charleston comprises three parts:

1. Three mandatory passes. Each player passes 3 tiles **right**, then **across**, then **left**. This is the first Charleston dance.
2. Three customary (optional) passes. Each player passes 3 tiles **left**, then **across**, then **right**. This is the second dance.
3. One final courtesy pass. Each player passes up to 3 tiles **across**.

Imagine you have a dance card with two names on it: Ralph (RALph) and Larry (LARry). The first dance, with RALph, is mandatory.

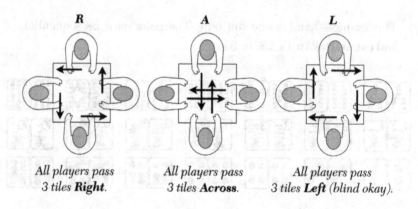

R	A	L

All players pass
3 tiles **Right**.

All players pass
3 tiles **Across**.

All players pass
3 tiles **Left** (blind okay).

You are permitted to "blind pass" 1, 2, or 3 tiles on the "first left," if you wish. No peeking! It's "blind"!

Any player is allowed to stop the Charleston at this point (and this point only).

The second dance, with LARry, occurs automatically, unless somebody stops dancing after the first dance with RALph. It's your privilege

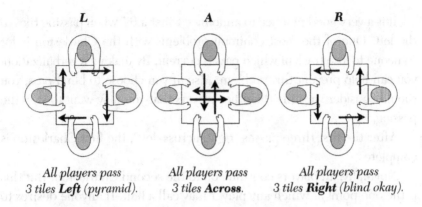

All players pass	*All players pass*	*All players pass*
3 tiles **Left** (pyramid).	3 tiles **Across**.	3 tiles **Right** (blind okay).

to stop the dance if you want to. Maybe RALph was "Mr. Right," in which case you don't need to dance with no stinking LARry! But once the second dance has begun, it cannot be stopped.

After the second Charleston, players optionally exchange 0, 1, 2, or 3 tiles with player opposite. A player never has to pass more tiles than she wants to on this "courtesy pass."

Let's examine the entire procedure in detail.

1.1. First, each player must choose 3 tiles from the hand. Take the 3 tiles off the rack, turn them facedown so nobody can see them, and pass them to the player at your right. You now have only 10 tiles (11, if you are the dealer) on your rack. And there are 3 facedown tiles at your left, from the player at your left. Take those 3 tiles and add them to your hand.

1.2. Next, each player must again choose 3 tiles from the hand. Take 3 tiles off the rack, turn them facedown, and pass them across the table. Place them within easy reach of your opposite. Take the 3 tiles she gives you, and place those on your rack.

1.3. Again, each player must choose 3 tiles to pass. But on the "first left," you are permitted to "blind pass," if you cannot spare 3 tiles from your rack. You can wait for the tiles from the player at your right, then take up to 3 of those *without looking at them*, and pass 3 tiles to your left.

It is a very good practice to announce, "first left," when passing tiles to the left. One of the most common problems with the Charleston is for someone to lose track of which pass is current. By making a verbalization, you can help prevent this problem. Also, if you choose to blind pass, you should consider warning the other players that you may want to stop the passing.

After the first three passes (right, across, left), the first Charleston is complete.

Normally, all players continue on to the second Charleston. But this is the one point at which any player may call a halt. If anyone desires to stop the passing now, she must so announce quickly. She must speak before any other player has picked up the next pass and put tiles on the rack.

2.1. Each player chooses 3 tiles to pass. On the "second left," it is customary to pile the third tile atop the other two, in a little pyramid shape. It is an extremely good practice to verbalize, saying, "second left," when placing the tile pyramid at your left side. Take the little pyramid at your right (passed to you by the player at your right), and place those tiles on your rack.

2.2. After having passed the "second left," all players must pass 3 tiles across. Pick 3 tiles from the hand, and pass them across. Place them within easy reach of your opposite. Take the 3 tiles she gives you, and place those on your rack.

2.3. Finally, all players must pass 3 tiles to the right. On the "last right," you may again (if needed) "blind pass." If you cannot spare 3 tiles from your rack, you can wait for the tiles from the player at your left, then take up to 3 of those *without looking at them*, and pass 3 tiles to your right. Take the 3 tiles from the player on your left, and put them on your rack.

After the second three passes (left, across, right), the second Charleston is complete. Now it is time for the final pass: the optional "Courtesy Pass."

3. Each player examines her tiles to see how many (3 tiles, 2 tiles, 1 tile, or 0 tiles) she wants to exchange with the opposite player. Talk to your opposite to determine how many tiles will be exchanged. If one of you wants to exchange fewer tiles than the other does, then it will be the lesser number that is exchanged. The Courtesy being optional, nobody has to pass more tiles than she wants to. Exchange the agreed-upon number of tiles, and put the received tiles on your rack.

The preliminaries are now finished. The game will begin.

Errors in the Charleston

If a player has picked up a 3-tile pass out of sequence, she should put them back and pick up the correct pass instead.

If the Charleston has gotten messed up and cannot be repaired, all players must throw in their tiles and start the deal over again.

If a player has passed tiles she didn't mean to pass, it's too bad. Once the next player has picked them up, it's too late.

If a player has passed a joker, it should be returned to her so she can pass a legal tile.

Keep the Charleston Moving!

The surest way to get everybody confused in the Charleston is to go slowly. In this intricate dance, you'll lose your footing if you think about it too much. You will learn to make the passes automatically, as long as it keeps moving along. But if someone takes too long to think, it is possible to get completely lost. If it cannot be remembered where the "dance" faltered so that all players can continue passing, then it's necessary to throw the tiles in, rebuild the walls, and start over. Nobody likes that.

So keep the Charleston moving. If you have two or three ways your hand might go, you have to choose one in a reasonable amount of time.

If you are a beginner and are having trouble passing tiles quickly enough, pay more attention to shaping the hand toward a section of the card, rather than toward a particular hand. Collecting tiles of a certain type (and discarding tiles of other types) will at least get you started toward making any of several different hands in a section. Once you have become more experienced, you will in due course have many of the hands memorized, which makes things go faster automatically.

LET THE GAME BEGIN

Having completed the Charleston phase, the play may now begin. The dealer is holding 14 tiles and the other three players are holding 13 tiles. Assuming the dealer cannot declare mah-jongg, she begins play by discarding 1 tile. She takes a tile from her hand and places it faceup at a random spot in the center of the table, announcing the name of the tile. Now she has 13 tiles like everybody else.

Play proceeds counterclockwise around the table in mah-jongg. After the dealer discards the first tile, the player to the dealer's right now takes her turn.

Picking & Discarding

On a player's turn, she takes a fourteenth tile into the hand (either by claiming a discard, or by picking from the wall). If the hand is not complete (does not match a hand on the card), she then discards a tile and says its name.

In the American game, discards are haphazardly placed on the discard floor (the space between the walls), in order that the players all pay attention, and to strategically hide what each player is doing.

Most of the time, a player does not want to claim the tile discarded by the player at her left. So most of the time, a player picks a tile from the wall. Most of the time, the picked tile does not complete the hand. So most of the time, the player discards a tile.

That's all there is to a turn—most of the time. Pick a tile, discard a tile.

Claiming a Discard

When someone's freshly discarded tile can be used by another player to complete a set, that other player can speak and take it. Remember, though, that mah-jongg is not rummy. You may not take a discard and conceal the tile in your hand (in a tournament, this is a punishable offense). When taking a discard, you must pay for the privilege by exposing the completed grouping atop the rack for all to see. Therefore, if you are not ready to make a completed grouping, you may not claim a discard at that time. But if a tile completes your hand, you may claim it any time and declare mah-jongg.

Exposable vs. Nonexposable Sets

It is not permitted to claim a discard to use in a pair, or to use as a single tile, except when doing so completes the hand immediately. The only kinds of sets that may be exposed prior to the mah-jongg declaration are pungs, kongs, quints, and sextets. But it *is* permitted to claim a discard for mah-jongg, regardless of the set size. Mah-jongging trumps melding.

To Make an Exposed Set (Pung, Kong, Quint, or Sextet)

If a player is working on a hand that requires four east wind tiles, and she has two easts and a joker, she is waiting for another east or a joker. If any other player at the table discards east, the player may verbally call for the tile and immediately expose the completed grouping atop her rack, no matter whose turn it is. Only the most recent discard is available for the taking, and only for a brief time (see "The Window of Opportunity," page 88).

The verbal call is important. It lets other players (who may be studying their tiles and their cards) know that something is happening, and they should look up. The NMJL rules do not specify what words must be said. It's usual to say, "I want that," or "Take," or "Call." It's important to speak clearly. Some players just say, "Um . . . ," but that's not a clear call. You have to express clearly and unequivocally your intention to take the discard, lest the next player pick from the wall before your window of opportunity closes. If it is your turn (if the discarder is the player at your left), then there is less urgency in making the verbalization. But it's still good manners to speak up so that players know that something important is happening.

In American mah-jongg, a discard may be claimed at any time by any player, regardless of whether it is that player's turn or not. As a result, it often happens that the order of play is interrupted. Players were previously taking turns, counterclockwise, picking from the wall and discarding.

Now someone is claiming a tile out of turn. She makes an exposure. And she discards a tile. The order of play having been disturbed, play now continues counterclockwise from her (from the player who took the discard and made the exposure). The player to her right picks and discards, and the normal turn-taking process proceeds from there.

New players sometimes think this is strange or somehow unfair, that any players between the discarder and the claimer "lose a turn." But that's not the way to look at it. The same rules apply to everyone, and everything evens out in the end.

The Window of Opportunity

When someone discards a tile that you need, you have to be quick, before the opportunity is lost forever. The next player will pick a tile and either rack it or discard. You have to speak up before that happens. There are clear rules for defining the "window of opportunity" in which you can claim a discard.

There are specific rules governing when a tile is "down" (and thus may be claimed) and when it is too late to claim it.

A tile is down the instant it is either named or it touches the table-top, whichever happens first. If a player, on her turn (after picking and racking), takes a tile off her rack and starts to name it, without finishing saying the tile's name and without touching the table with it, the tile is not yet down. But the instant it touches, or it is completely named, the tile is down, and available for claiming by another player.

The window of opportunity is now open. The most recent discard may be claimed by any player . . . until the window closes.

Normally, the next player (the player to the right of the discarder) now reaches, takes the tile from the end of the wall, and looks at it. The window of opportunity is still open (her looking at the tile does *not* close the window of opportunity). The player holding the picked tile might rack it (closing the window of opportunity) or she might discard it (closing the window of opportunity) or she might declare mah-jongg (closing the window of opportunity). While the window is open, another player may claim the previous discard, and the picked tile would have to go back on the wall. Once the window has closed, though, the discarded tile is "dead."

The current live discard "covers" the old discard, and all previous discards. Only the current live discard may be claimed, and only while the window is open.

To Go Mah-Jongg

Throughout most of the game, each player's hand contains 13 tiles. A complete mah-jongg hand is 14 tiles. When a player's 13-tile hand is complete except for 1 particular tile, and no tile in the hand can be discarded without ruining the hand, the hand is said to be "calling" or "waiting."

Let's say the player is holding a calling hand, needing only a North Wind. If someone discards north, the player must speak up quickly. The calling player should say "Mah-Jongg," take the tile, and immediately expose the completed hand atop her rack.

Especially when it is not your turn, it is important that you verbalize the call. Say "Mah-Jongg," or "Maj," or "That's it." It's important to speak up, lest the next player pick from the wall before your window of opportunity closes.

"I Picked It!"

The player might pick the winning tile herself. I recommend that you announce, "I picked it," then expose the completed hand atop your rack.

When Somebody Wins

When someone has gone mah-jongg, the game is over. All players cease playing, examine the winner's hand to verify that it's valid, and settle up. The nonwinning players pay chips or coins to the winner. Only one player can win a hand of mah-jongg! Then the players throw in all their tiles, which are then shuffled and built into a new wall for another game. The next player will deal this time.

When Somebody Else Wins

Hold the kvetching! The winner deserves the limelight before you can take the stage. Of course you want to tell everybody the sad story of how close you came, or how bad your tiles were. But when somebody wins, your first duty is to the winner. Watch as she exposes her hand. Make sure you know what hand she made, and that it's valid, and how much you owe her. Then pay her. Then you can share your sob story about your hand.

When Nobody Wins

It often happens that the wall runs out of tiles without anyone declaring mah-jongg. When this happens, nobody wins. Throw in the tiles, shuffle them, build a new wall, and play another game. The next player (counterclockwise from the previous dealer) will deal this time.

JOKERS ARE WILD . . . WITH LIMITS

Jokers are wild, and may be used to represent any tile (suit tile, wind, dragon, or flower), in any pung, kong, quint, or sextet. A pung is 3 identical tiles. A kong is 4 identical tiles. A quint is 5 identical tiles. A sextet is 6 identical tiles. If the National Mah Jongg League reintroduces larger sets of identical tiles, such as septettes or octettes, then jokers could be used in those as well.

Jokers may never be used in a pair or to represent a single tile. A NEWS is a grouping made of 4 single, nonidentical wind tiles (it is not a kong). And a 2007 is not a kong (it's a grouping made of 2 singles and a pair). So jokers may not be used in a NEWS grouping or a 2007 grouping.

A player may use multiple jokers in an exposure. It is not necessary to have a natural tile in the hand prior to claiming a discard to make an exposure. For instance, the player might have three jokers, and claim someone's discarded 1B (One Bam), and make an exposed kong using three jokers and the 1B, without previously having had any natural 1B tiles.

A player need not have any natural tiles in a set that's contained fully within the hand (a set that's not revealed until making mah-jongg). The player might use four jokers in a kong of N's (North Wind tiles), for example, without having any natural N's in the hand at all.

Jokers May Be Redeemed

When a player has made an exposure that contains a joker, any player may replace the joker with the natural tile that the joker represents, and take the joker into her hand. This is called "redeeming" the joker. Some people call it "exchanging."

There are clear rules governing joker redemption:

1. A joker may be redeemed during a player's turn, after first bringing a fourteenth tile into the hand, either by using a discard to make an exposure or by picking a tile from the wall. After redeeming the joker, if the player cannot claim mah-jongg, the player must discard a tile. A player may not redeem a joker before bringing in the fourteenth tile or after discarding.
2. A player is permitted to redeem multiple jokers on multiple racks during her turn.
3. A player may redeem a joker atop her own rack.
4. It is not necessary to expose any sets that may be completed by a redeemed joker. Redeeming a joker is not the same thing as using a discarded tile.
5. It is perfectly okay to redeem a joker if the player is making a concealed hand (a hand marked "C" on the card). Redeeming a joker is not the same thing as using a discarded tile.
6. It is okay to redeem a joker from a dead player's hand, provided that the joker had been exposed properly. Improperly exposed jokers are returned to the dead player's hand anyway, where they are safely removed from temptation. There is more on joker validity and improper exposure in the section on dead hands (page 101).
7. There is no such thing as "reverse redemption." A player may never put a joker on anyone's rack in order to take a natural tile.

Jokers May Be Discarded

Novices are often amazed to learn that jokers may be discarded, and that experienced players discard them all the time. Because many hands on the card contain numerous pairs and single tiles (which may never utilize jokers), it frequently happens that a player obtains a joker that she cannot use.

Discarding jokers can also be a strategic move, called "dogging." It's used toward the end of a game when a player realizes she cannot win. Once a joker is discarded, it is considered a dead tile. *Nobody can claim it and use it for any purpose whatsoever.* Because a joker cannot be taken once discarded, it's always a safe discard.

The practice when discarding a joker is to call it the same as the previous discard. For instance, player one discards 1B and says "One Bam." Player two picks, then discards a joker, and says "Same." Or she might say "One Bam." This is done for strategic reasons, and to encourage other players to pay attention with their eyes as well as their ears.

Although the player is saying the name of a nonjoker tile, the discarded joker may not be taken for any purpose whatsoever. Likewise, the previously discarded tile is no longer available for the taking. In the example in the previous paragraph, the 1B tile is covered by the discarded joker, and both are considered dead tiles.

The rules governing discarded jokers also govern discarded redeemable tiles. For instance, player one has an exposure of three E's and one joker. Player two discards E. Player three wishes she could take the discarded E and exchange it for the joker on player one's rack, but the rules do not permit this. If player three has three jokers, she may call for the discarded E and make her own kong of E atop her own rack, but that is the only use that may be made of the discarded E in such a case.

When a joker or a redeemable tile has been discarded, because the rules do not permit taking either one, and because most people covet jokers, the usual response is to tear out one's hair and scream to the heavens, "Oh! I wanted that!"

Jokerless Bonus

All the hands on the NMJL card, except the hands in the Singles And Pairs section, contain at least one pung or kong (a set in which a joker may be used). If a player succeeds in making a hand without jokers, then a bonus is earned. The hand's score is doubled.

Since the hands in the Singles And Pairs section do not contain any pungs or kongs, quints or sextets, the jokerless bonus does not apply to the Singles And Pairs hands.

Joker History

The use of jokers has gone through an evolutionary process in American mah-jongg. Until 1961, the American game did not have jokers at all. Flowers were wild, and the number of flowers fluctuated between eight and twenty-four. After joker tiles were introduced into the American game in 1961, the number of flowers and jokers fluctuated for several years, finally stabilizing at eight flowers and eight jokers ten years later, in the 1971–72 card.

Wild tiles could be used for any part of the hand at first. Around 1984, a rule was introduced that jokers could not be used for singles or pairs.

If you buy an older mah-jongg set, it might not come with eight jokers. It might come with extra flowers. And sometimes you might meet an older player who hasn't played for many years, who doesn't know the current joker rules.

SCORING & PAYMENT

American mah-jongg is typically played as a low-stakes gambling game. So when a player wins, she receives payment from the other players in coins. The hand values given on the NMJL card range from 25 to 50 points (25 to 50 cents).

Somebody always pays double. There are only two ways you can win: by discard or by self-pick. If you take a discard to win, the discarder pays double; nondiscarders pay single value. If you pick it yourself, everybody pays double. Winning by redeeming a joker is regarded to be the same as self-pick.

The score is doubled again if the hand has no jokers (not including the hands in the Singles and Pairs section of the card). Complete scoring information is on the back of the card.

So if you win by discard, jokerless, the discarder pays double double (four times the value of the hand). For the math-impaired, here is an example of scoring a win by discard: Alice discards red. Betty says "Maj." Betty shows her tiles, and it's a hand composed of pungs, kongs, and/or quints, with or without pairs (it is *not* a hand from the Singles And Pairs section of the card), and it doesn't have any jokers. Betty announces her score. "It's a 25-point hand, and it's jokerless. So it's double, 50 cents, for you two. But Alice owes me double, since she threw it—a dollar." Charlene and Delores both pay 50 cents, and Alice pays $1. If Esther bet on Alice, everybody (except Betty, of course) also pays Esther (exactly the same amount they each paid Betty)—for more on betting, see the following.

And here's an example of scoring a win by self-pick: Alice has an exposure, One Bams with a joker. Betty's hand is waiting, and a joker would give her the win. It's a 25-point hand. She has no jokers in the hand, and hopes to pick a natural tile for a jokerless win. Alice discards a joker. Betty gnashes her teeth at Alice's audacity (wasting a perfectly good joker like that) and reaches for the wall. She picks—it's a One Bam. She exchanges it for Alice's exposed joker and says, "I picked it. Fifty all." Everyone pays Betty 50 cents. If it had been jokerless, everyone would pay $1 (25 doubled twice equals 100), but it's not good strategy to pass up a chance to go mah-jongg.

It is the winner's duty to tell the other players how much they must pay her. If she undervalues her hand, the official rules say that no other player should offer any advice to the winner about how to score the hand properly. But when the players are friendly with one another, it's fairly common to help the winner with her math, if she seems to need it. When playing in a tournament, it's best to let the winner do all her own math, as long as she doesn't overvalue the hand.

Pie

A "pie" is a limit on the amount that a player can lose during an evening's play. Most West Coast players play with a $5 pie—which means that each player brings a coin purse with exactly $5 in coins. When the player's coins are all gone, she continues to play—at no additional risk. Legend has it that rich East Coast ladies play with a $10 pie, and there are some devil-may-care heavy gamblers who play without a pie.

As for the etymology of the term, have you ever seen a pie chart? That's a circular representation of something that can be broken down into percentages. So in American mah-jongg, the term means "I have this much pie to go aROUND, and when it's gone, nobody eats any more pie."

Chips

It isn't always kosher to pay one another with coins, especially when playing mah-jongg in a public area where big-time gambling might attract the unwanted attention of Johnny Law. So in such cases (or when players simply don't actually want to gamble their hard-earned quarters

*Some sets come with big poker chips (left). Some sets come with
smaller round chips with square holes (center). Traditional Chinese
mah-jongg chips are scoring sticks with dots painted on (right).*

away), chips may be used instead. Then if you want to play for money,
settle up at the end of the entire play session.

When using any kind of chips, simply allocate them to any appropriate denominations that work for you. For example, you might break
down your chips as follows:

- Blue chips are worth 50 cents (four per player=$2)
- Red chips are worth 25 cents (eight per player=$2)
- Green, white, and yellow chips are all worth 10 cents (ten per
  player=$1)

It's rare for sets to come with the perfect number of chips of the
perfect number of denominations to make an elegant distribution. It's
okay to improvise. It might even be fun to play with Monopoly money
instead of chips or coins. "I picked it! Fork over fifty big ones, ladies!"

Tournament Scoring

In a tournament, coins are not used. Rather, score is kept on a paper
scorecard. Each tournament sets its own scoring system, but it's usual
simply to award points to the winner, and not subtract points from nonwinners except when discarding to two or more exposures, or for being
late (thus doing harm to the other players at the table).

Example:

Going mah-jongg	Card value
Self-pick	+10 points
Jokerless	+20 points
Wall game	10 points
Throwing win to two exposures	-10 points
Throwing win to three exposures	-25 points
Not being in seat at game start	-25 points
Nonwinner (someone else won)	0 points
Dead hand	0 points

A thorough tournament organizer also has a policy on how to penalize certain errors that may occur, such as misnaming a discard (when this results in a mishap) or throwing in the hand prematurely.

After a hand has been played, each player's points are noted on the table's scorecard. After four hands (one round) have been played, the players' scores are added and the scorecard is delivered to the tournament scorekeeper.

The winner of the tournament is the player whose overall score for all rounds is the highest.

ERRORS & CONFLICTS

Errors are inevitable. The official rules cover what to do in most common error situations, and some general principles cover what to do in uncommon error situations. Conflicts are also inevitable. The rules govern what to do in most cases, and there are some principles that can be used to resolve most other cases.

Conflicting Claims

The rules handle how to resolve multiple claims for a discarded tile. When two players want the same discard for exposure (to make a meld, not to go mah-jongg) or two players want the same discard for mah-jongg, the player whose turn would ordinarily come first in line after the discarder gets the tile. It isn't a race to speak first. As long as both calls were voiced within a reasonably short period of time, the player next in line from the discarder gets the tile.

For example, let's say player one throws a tile, and player three and player four both want it. Player three's turn would normally come before player four's turn, so player three gets the tile.

When one player wants the discard for exposure and the other player wants it for mah-jongg, of course the mah-jongg call trumps the exposure call. It's not a race to speak first, but the calls must be voiced within a reasonably short period of time, and before someone exposes.

Erroneous Discard

When a player realizes she has discarded a tile she didn't mean to, she may not take it back if she has said the tile's name in full or if she has touched the tile to the table. Once either of those has occurred, the tile is down and may not be taken back. Player erred, and she must live with the consequences.

Sometimes a player misspeaks, saying the name of a different tile than the one she discarded. The player must correctly speak the name of the tile she actually discarded. The tile may not be taken back—"down is down." The game may resume once the player has said the correct name of the tile lying on the discard floor; another player may call the correctly named tile for exposure.

If, however, another player declares mah-jongg on the miscalled discard, the game ends. The player who declared mah-jongg collects four times the value of her hand from the erring player alone.

Erroneous Call for Exposure

As long as the player has not yet exposed tiles from her hand, she may retract her verbal call for the current discard. Calling for a discard, picking it up, and even racking it (putting it atop the flat portion of her rack) are all retractable actions, with no penalty. If she exposes tiles from her hand, though, she commits to making the exposure. She must take the discard and expose tiles from her hand, even if doing so results in her hand going dead.

If a player has exposed a pung and wishes to change it to a kong (or vice versa), she may do this only prior to discarding a tile. Once a player has made an exposure and discarded, the exposure may not be changed.

If a player has made a bad exposure (such as mixing flowers and One Bams), she may only fix it (by removing the inappropriate tiles from the exposure) prior to discarding a tile. Once a player has made an exposure and discarded, the exposure may not be changed.

Erroneous Mah-Jongg

A player errs in declaring mah-jongg if the hand she displays is not on the card, or doesn't properly match the requirements for the hand as shown on the card. For instance, one of the most common types of "false maj" is to use the wrong suit composition (due to having misread the color-coding on the card). When the player has declared mah-jongg, it is her duty to explain the hand, indicating which hand on the card it is, and how much each player owes her. It is the duty of the other players to verify that the hand is correct. If anyone can demonstrate that the hand is incorrect, the erring player's hand is declared dead, her freshly exposed tiles are returned to the sloping front of her rack, and the other players continue playing. At least, that's what happens most of the time.

There are several problems that can result from an erroneous declaration of mah-jongg. One error can result in a cascade of further errors, if the other players do not follow the proper procedures (verifying the validity of the hand before throwing in their own hands, or destroying the wall looking for their maj tile).

Penalties vary depending on the fallout from the original error.

Erroneous Maj Call, Quickly Withdrawn

If a player declares mah-jongg but withdraws the declaration without exposing her hand and without causing any sort of cascade of further errors on the part of other players, no harm has been done, no penalty is incurred, and the game may continue.

Erroneous Maj Exposure, Without Further Errors

If a player declares mah-jongg and exposes the hand without resulting in another player destroying her own hand or the wall, and it is realized that the hand is erroneous, her hand is declared dead. Her freshly exposed tiles are returned to the sloping front of her rack, and the others continue playing. She is subject to payment for mah-jongg to the winner, same as if she hadn't been declared dead.

Erroneous Maj, with Cascading Error(s)

If a player declares mah-jongg and another player throws in her hand before the maj is discovered to be erroneous, two hands are declared dead. The two remaining live players continue playing. If one of them wins, all three other players (including the two dead players) pay the winner.

If a player declares mah-jongg and another player destroys the wall before the maj is discovered to be erroneous, the hand has ended. The player who destroyed the wall must pay the value of the cheapest hand on the card (usually 25) to the two live players.

If a player declares mah-jongg, exposes the hand, and two players throw in their hands before the discovery of the erroneous maj, the player whose maj call started the cascade of errors is at fault. She alone pays the surviving player (the one whose hand was not thrown in), double the value of the hand she declared maj on. Example: if the player had declared maj on a hand listed on the card as being worth 25 points, and the hand was then determined to be erroneous after two players threw in their own hands, she must pay the lone nonerring player 50 points. The tiles are all thrown in and shuffled.

Change of Heart

Players often change their minds after making a verbalization or a move. Sometimes such calls or moves may be rescinded, per the following.

- **Passing**—A Charleston pass cannot be rescinded once the recipient of the pass has picked it up. It's bad manners to take back a pass when the recipient is in the act of reaching to pick it up.
- **Picking**—A player can decide not to take a tile from the wall (and instead pick up the current discard) only if she has not yet lifted the tile from the wall. Merely touching the tile does not commit her to keeping it.
- **Discarding**—A player cannot take back a discard if she has said the tile's name in full *or* touched the tile to the table. "Down is down."

- **Taking a Discard**—A player may withdraw an exposure call, if she has not yet exposed tiles from her hand. Picking up a discarded tile is a rescindable act, even if she has put it on her rack, as long as nobody else has yet seen tiles from her hand.
- **Exposure Size**—A player may change the number of tiles in her exposure only before she discards, ending her turn. If a player calls a tile, exposes 3 tiles from her hand, then realizes that her exposure should be a pung instead of a kong, she is permitted to put 1 tile back in her hand (she's allowed to change the kong to a pung, or vice versa) up until the moment she discards. Once her turn is over, the exposure may never be added to or subtracted from.
- **Winning**—A player can withdraw a spoken mah-jongg claim only if she has not yet exposed tiles from her hand and nobody else has made a fatal error as a result of the vocal mah-jongg claim. Picking up a discard, and even putting it atop her rack, does not commit her to keeping it.
- **Death Challenge**—Once someone has called another player dead, or even asked if another player is dead, the death challenge may not be withdrawn.

Death

A hand can go dead through a player's error or through circumstances beyond the player's control. When a hand can be seen by other players to be dead, the hand can be called dead by any other player at the table. A player may make a "death challenge" for a number of reasons:

- **No Such Hand:** Player's exposures do not match any hand on the current card.
- **Unwinnable:** Player's exposures indicate that player needs to make a pair, and 3 or more of the needed tiles are dead on the table.
- **Exposed Concealed Hand:** Player's exposures indicate that player's hand must be concealed.
- **Too Many or Too Few Tiles:** Player is holding 12 or fewer tiles (13 or fewer after picking), or player is holding 15 or more tiles (14 or more between turns), once the Charleston has ended and the dealer has begun play.
- **Rule Violation:** Players may be called dead for picking out of

turn, for putting a called tile into the hand instead of atop the rack, or for certain other actions. In tournaments, such violations are immediately punishable. In home games, players may optionally be let off with friendly warnings. Repeat violators are subject to the appropriate penalty.

When any player observes that another player's hand is dead, she is allowed to call the hand dead. Some players try to hedge their bets by asking if the hand is dead; this amounts to the same thing. Vocalizing a death challenge or a death query has the same result: all eyes turn to the challenged hand.

The player on the receiving end of a death challenge must either acknowledge that she is indeed dead, or deny it (without explaining what hand she is making). Then the game continues, either with or without that player, depending on her reply to the challenge.

If a player has erroneously issued a death challenge, or if a player has erroneously denied a death challenge (which can be determined at the end of the hand), the erring player must pay value of the cheapest hand on the card (25) to the other player.

For example, if Abigail calls Betty dead, and Betty denies it, they play out the hand, then check Betty's hand to see who was right. If Abigail was wrong (Betty's hand wasn't dead), she owes Betty 25. If Betty was wrong (her hand had indeed been dead), then she owes Abigail 25.

It's not recommended that you call yourself dead. You are supposed to play defensively until someone else calls you dead (and this is the wisest course, strategically speaking). If you happen to blurt out that you are dead, you aren't officially dead yet (you haven't been called dead, so you cannot stop playing), you must continue playing until somebody obligingly calls you dead.

When a player is called dead due to an erroneous exposure, the tiles in the erring exposure should be returned to the rack. This removes any unredeemable jokers from temptation.

Dead Hands & Joker Redemption—The Principle

Jokers that were exposed properly remain valid for redemption after a player has been declared dead and has acknowledged the validity of the death challenge. If you make a kong, nobody has enough information about which hand you're making, so you can't be declared dead on the basis of that exposure alone. Any jokers in that kong are live, and stay alive even if you are declared dead later.

Jokers that were exposed improperly are not available for redemption. Let's say that your first exposure was a kong of 4's (with a joker) and your second exposure was a kong of dragons (with a joker). Let's say that the card does not have a hand that allows kongs of 4's and dragons (let's imagine that the hand is clearly not anywhere on the card). Anybody could now declare you dead, based on your improper second exposure.

Any jokers that had been exposed prior to the blunder (the jokers in the first exposure) are still valid for redemption, but any jokers exposed in the course of making the blunder (the jokers in the second exposure) are dead. All portions of the hand exposed erroneously are to be returned to the rack, including and especially the now-dead jokers.

It sometimes occurs that an error (for instance, too many or too few tiles in the hand) is not discovered until some time later (so that the exact timing of the error and any joker exposures is not known or cannot be determined). When this happens, jokers exposed *prior to* the discovery/announcement of the error remain alive for redemption purposes, and jokers exposed concurrent with the announcement of a problem are dead and should be returned to the rack.

Dead Hands and Joker Redemption—Specific Cases

In addition to proper/improper exposure, joker validity can also depend on the player's cause of death.

- **No Such Hand:** It usually takes multiple exposures before players can discern that the player is playing an erroneous hand. After making a first exposure, the hand's rescue is still within the realm of possibility. In such cases, any jokers exposed prior to the discovery of the error are alive for redemption. When subsequent exposures reveal that the hand is not valid, any jokers in those subsequent exposures are dead—and those subsequent exposures should be returned to the rack. Occasionally a hand's nonvalidity can be determined upon the first exposure. For instance, if the player's first exposure is a quint of dragons and if the current card does not have any hand using a dragon quint. In such an instance, all the exposed tiles (including any jokers) are returned to the rack.

- **Exposed Concealed Hand:** Upon death declaration due to exposing a hand that was supposed to be concealed, all tiles (including jokers) are returned to the rack. See rule 3(b), page 16, of the official rule book.

- **Unwinnable:** Jokers exposed prior to the death declaration remain alive for redemption. If jokers are exposed concurrently with the discovery of the hand's unwinnability, those jokers are dead and should be returned to the rack (together with other tiles that were in the act of being exposed at that time).

- **Too Many or Too Few Tiles:** Jokers exposed prior to the discovery and announcement of the error remain alive for redemption, if it cannot be determined when the error occurred. Jokers exposed concurrently with the discovery and announcement of the error are not redeemable, and should be returned to the rack (together with other tiles that were in the act of being exposed at that time).

- **Rule Violation:** Jokers exposed prior to the death challenge for a rule violation remain alive for redemption.

ETIQUETTE & TABLE PRACTICES

During the course of a game of American mah-jongg, there are certain practices that are normally followed. Players all across America use the same practices.

Use of Racks

American players use racks to line up the walls, to hold the tiles of the hand, to push the walls, and to place exposures. In olden times, when American players played for chips, racks even held the chips.

Use of Racks in Building Walls

Once the tiles have been turned facedown and shuffled, each player takes some tiles at random and lines them up along the back of her rack, two tiles high. Because the standard length of racks was determined before the National Mah Jongg League standardized the American game at 8 flowers and 8 jokers (152 tiles), most racks are not quite long enough to line up nineteen stacks without extending beyond the end of the rack. It's normal for the wall to be 1 or 2 tiles longer than the rack. Some players take the extra stack and use them to make a "tail," which is then placed perpendicular to the wall at the dealer's left, like a stubby "T." This is a nonstandard practice, so details are not given here. You may follow any procedure that your group likes. Most players just make walls longer than the racks. After the wall has been built, the player should run her hand along the wall to smooth it out and straighten it.

Use of Racks for Holding the Tiles

The rack has a sloping front. After the tiles have been dealt to the players, each player arranges her tiles on the sloping front of the rack. This arrangement makes it easy to read the faces of the tiles.

Use of Racks for Pushing the Wall

In American mah-jongg, it is customary to leave three walls lined up along racks (parallel to the edges of the table), and one wall angled into the center of the table. As one wall is depleted and another wall comes into play, it is good manners to serve the wall out into the center of the table. The rack is used to keep the wall straight during this procedure. The rack remains in place at the left end—the right end is swung in toward the center of the table. This applies equally to the dealing process.

During the game, when it becomes a player's turn to serve the wall, there's a minor difficulty. Because the player's tiles are on her rack, it can be tricky to swing the wall out and not reveal her tiles to the player on her right. There are four standard ways of serving the wall without revealing one's goodies.

1. You can use the card to cover your tiles. Holding the card with your thumb and index finger of both hands at the ends, put the card over the tiles. Then, extending your other fingers to the rack, and holding the card and the rack simultaneously, swing the right

end of the rack (using the left end, the end with the chip prongs, as a hinge) to the center of the table. Pull back the rack, leaving the wall of tiles in place. This maneuver can be tricky if the wall of tiles is longer than the rack itself. Therefore some players habitually place the last one or two stacks out into the table (on the back end of the dwindling wall already there) prior to pushing the wall out.

2. The more elegant method is to use your left arm to cover your tiles and push out the rack. Placing your left elbow at the left end of the rack, extending your left forearm along the face of the rack, and holding the right end of the rack with your right hand, push the rack out (without pushing the left end forward), then pull back the rack (leaving the tiles in place).

3. Some unwise players use the honor method. They find the above techniques too difficult to master. They don't conceal the tiles at all, pushing the rack right on out there and trusting the player on the right not to look at their tiles. This method is not

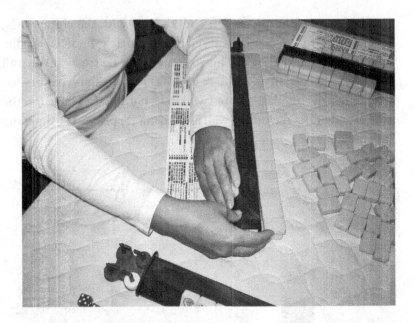

recommended. There is no rule against a player looking at a tile shown her by another (unwise) player.

4. If the set is equipped with "helping hands," no special technique is needed. Simply grab the little knob at the right end of the swinging arm and push out.

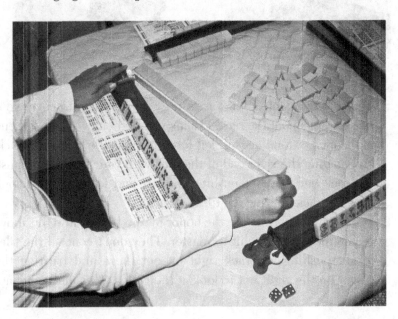

Timing is important. In order not to slow down the game, don't push out the wall on your own turn, and don't do it while another player is reaching out her hand to take the end tile. Pay attention, and when it's your turn to serve the wall, don't wait for someone else to remind you.

Use of Racks for Displaying Exposures & the Completed Hand

Modern American racks have a horizontal surface that is used for displaying exposures and the completed hand.

When calling for a discard to make an exposure prior to going mah-jongg, it's customary to put the first one at the left side of the rack, then subsequent exposures to the right (in chronological order, not the order shown on the card).

When displaying the completed hand for others to examine and verify, it's polite and customary to arrange the sets in the same order as they appear on the card. And to explain which hand it is.

VERBALIZATIONS DURING PLAY

American mah-jongg is not a quiet game. The game requires the use of certain verbalizations. Players must speak when claiming a discard for exposure or mah-jongg, when declaring mah-jongg, and when discarding a tile. Speak clearly and with sufficient volume so all can hear. Players may be talking, so it's your job to make sure your voice is heard.

Calling for Exposure & Declaring Mah-Jongg

It's required that the player speak up clearly when requesting the current discard, either to make an exposure or to complete the hand.

When taking the discard for exposure, it's not necessary to say if the call is for pung, kong, quint, or sextet. It's necessary only to express clearly a desire to take the tile. Most people say "Call" or "Take." It's also acceptable to say, "I want that," or any other clear expression of a desire to take the tile.

When taking the discard for mah-jongg, it's important to express clearly that the tile completes the hand. Most people say "Mah-jongg" or its diminutive, "Maj." It's also acceptable and recommended to say instead, "That's it."

When declaring mah-jongg by self-pick, it's polite and customary to say, "I picked it," and show the tile that completed the hand.

When making mah-jongg, it's polite and customary to calculate the score aloud and point to each player, clearly informing her how much she is to pay you.

Announcing Tile Names

It is required in American mah-jongg to announce the name of the tile as you discard it. These are the names of the tiles under the American system:

One Bam	One Crak	One Dot	North
Two Bam	Two Crak	Two Dot	East
Three Bam	Three Crak	Three Dot	West
Four Bam	Four Crak	Four Dot	South
Five Bam	Five Crak	Five Dot	Soap*
Six Bam	Six Crak	Six Dot	Green
Seven Bam	Seven Crak	Seven Dot	Red
Eight Bam	Eight Crak	Eight Dot	Flower**
Nine Bam	Nine Crak	Nine Dot	Joker***

* "Soap" is the most common nickname for a white dragon. It is also acceptable to say, "White" or "Zero."

** When discarding a flower, one never says the number on the flower tile—one never says the season name if the flower tile is so marked, or says "Animal" or "Person in flowing robes" or "Rickshaw," etc. The only proper thing to say when discarding a flower is "Flower," regardless of what is depicted or written on the tile.

*** When discarding a joker, it is the usual practice to say "Same" or to repeat the name of the previous discard. Some people say "Ditto" or "Likewise." The reason for this practice goes back to a now outdated rule, but it's mainly done to keep other players on their toes (to force them to keep their eyes open, not only their ears). No player may ever claim a discarded joker, and no player may ever claim a nonjoker named upon the discard of a joker. When discarding a joker, it is acceptable to say "Joker."

For the sake of harmonious play, it is best not to deviate from this naming system when playing with American players.

The name of the tile is spoken at about the same time that you place the tile on the table. The moment the tile is either completely named or it touches the table, it is considered "down." This consideration (exactly when the tile is "down") is important for players wanting to claim a discard or draw from the wall.

OTHER ETIQUETTE POINTERS

Keep the game moving!

Keep your hands behind your rack. There's nothing more annoying than having the dead discards obscured by the resting hand of a player who thinks it's a good idea to rest her wrist on her rack.

When picking, pull the tile toward you before looking at it. There is nothing to stop other players from looking at your tile if you look at the tile in the center of the table.

Some players think that it's smart, upon hearing the previous discard, to quickly pick and immediately rack the next wall tile, because the tile might be a joker, and closing the window of opportunity rapidly (so the theory usually goes) ensures one of keeping it. But that isn't smart—it's ungracious and aggressive. This practice, which can be called "pick & rack," makes it extremely difficult for anyone to claim the current live discard. If everybody did that, only inhumanly fast robots could ever call a discard! Best to wait a beat before picking. Then, having paused a beat before picking, if you're that worried about the 5 percent odds of it being a joker, go ahead and rack it quickly. The odds are 95 percent against it being a joker. And besides, that isn't the only tile you could want. Most of the time, a tile you want can also be called for exposure anyway.

When you're the dealer, after you roll the dice it's your job to pick up the dice. Place them in the corner of the table at your right.

Don't talk to bettors or bystanders.

Pay attention. Look at tiles when discarded. Never ask, "Where is it" or "What was it?" Look at the winner's hand when she exposes it and know which hand on the card it is, before she throws it in and before you begin telling your sad tale of woe about your hand. After the winner throws it in, never ask, "What hand was it" or "Who threw it?"

And lastly, don't try to enforce etiquette on others. It only annoys them and makes them defensive. Do your best to act courteously, but it's best not to proselytize.

C. How to Win

Strategy is a many-faceted topic. Strategy begins with the way one shapes the hand during the Charleston as trends appear. Strategy is needed to choose what to discard and what to call. Strategy is involved in defense, based on what other players discard and call. Even whether or not to use, redeem, or discard jokers requires strategic thinking. Defense, offense, body language—all are examined herein. But before those specifics are examined, it's important to consider the biggest common mistake novice players make.

NOVICE PLAYERS' BIGGEST COMMON MISTAKE

Most novices, having learned the game, find it very difficult to get into a game with experienced players. The reason for this is easy to understand: experienced players take the game seriously, they want an enjoyable play session that doesn't drag on, and they don't want to have to answer beginner questions.

The biggest mistake most novice players make is to value winning over just keeping up. When you are not yet an experienced player, remember: *It is more important to avoid disruption of the game than it is to win.* If you want to be invited back to play again, you need to keep the game moving. It can't all be about you, right from day one. The other players want to enjoy the game, too . . . and they outnumber you.

If you find yourself struggling with a jumble of disassociated tiles and an inscrutable card too long, the others will start to cough, roll their eyes, and drum their fingernails impatiently. If you find this happening to you, you must make a self-sacrificing move.

Pass any three tiles. Just try not to let any more fingernails drum, any more eyes roll, any more throats to tighten into subtle coughs. After sacrificing like this a while, eventually you'll get a hand with which you can win. It takes patience and self-control. The beginner who competitively obsesses on winning is bound to slow the game down. You might win a few times, but you won't be invited back to play again.

Strive for harmony. Go with the flow. Relax, be patient, and the winning will come in time. Skill and winning come with practice. Be patient with yourself.

CHARLESTON STRATEGY—HOW TO CHOOSE WHICH TILES TO PASS

For beginners, one of the most difficult aspects of learning the American game is in learning an effective strategy for the Charleston. The Charleston is a crucial phase of the American game. Passing tiles gives you an excellent head start if you do it right. Two things to consider during the Charleston are offense and defense.

Collect Tiles for Your Hand (Offense)

Look at the tiles you received in the deal. Usually, you have 13 tiles. If you're the dealer, you have 14. Look for pairs and triples first, and see if they suggest a particular section of the card. If not, see if any of the singles do.

- For example, perhaps you have numerous even-numbered tiles. If so, you should concentrate on the 2468 (even-numbered hands) section of the card. So pass odd-numbered tiles and winds.
- If your hand has a lot of odd-numbered suit tiles, consider going for the 13579 section (pass even numbered tiles and wind tiles).
- If you have several wind tiles, perhaps you should focus on the Winds and Dragons section of the card. Pass suit tiles that do not help make hands in that area.
- If you have numerous jokers, consider going for a Quint hand. If you have no jokers, consider going for a Singles And Pairs hand.
- If your hand has 3's, 6's, and 9's, go for the 369 section.
- If your hand has a lot of low (1 through 5) or high (5 through 9) numbered suit tiles, consider going for a Consecutive Run hand (pass wind tiles; pass high tiles if you're collecting low; pass low tiles if you're collecting high). And so on.

- It often happens that your tiles do not suggest a clear direction. When this happens, see if your tiles might suggest multiple different hands.

Having assessed the hand, use the process of elimination. Determine which tiles are not needed for any of your possible target hands. You need to find three to pass.

During the first Charleston, you will receive tiles from each player. You will get an idea of what kind of tiles are being passed. During the second Charleston, you will usually see more of the same old tiles. So if your hand is not coming together during the first Charleston, you should consider changing what kind of hand you want to go for, and use a different strategy in the second Charleston, based on the tiles that are being passed.

You will also be able to get an idea of what tiles are *not* going around. Knowing that, you know which hands *not* to pursue. But don't spend too much time thinking—other players want to keep the Charleston moving.

Be Careful You Don't Give a Hand to an Opponent (Defense)

Some players put this defensive consideration first (ahead of building the hand), but that's not the secret to winning. Don't forget that during the Charleston, not only are you collecting tiles from your opponents, they are collecting tiles from you. So you want to be mindful of some general principles when passing tiles to others.

- Never pass a joker. It's actually against the rules.
- Try to avoid passing 3 related tiles (3 winds, 3 dragons, 3 of a kind, all even numbers, etc.).
- Try not to pass flowers unless you have to.
- Pay attention to what the other player does with the tiles you pass. Does she groan in dismay and pass them on, or does she place them on her rack and keep them? You can learn a lot about what the other players are doing if you just pay attention.
- Try to remember what kind of tiles you passed to a player, and don't pass the same kind to that player again.

- Try to remember which tiles you passed and determine which ones do not come back. Someone kept them. Try to figure out who, if you can. It's kind of like the old shell game. Try not to pass that kind of tile anymore.

MORE BEGINNER STRATEGY & TIPS

- Practice with the card before joining other players at a table. Using your own tiles, try building all the hands on the card. Build each hand different ways (using different suit combinations and, if the hand permits, different number combinations).
- Play a mah-jongg tile-matching game on the computer. There are free ones you can download from the Internet. Playing these games makes it easier to spot tiles among a crowd of tiles (a skill that becomes handy when reading the discards).
- Back fold the card so it lies flat, and tuck the top of the card under your rack so the card doesn't overhang the edge of the table. If your sleeve catches the card edge when reaching for the wall, the card will flip, and possibly reveal some of your tiles.
- It can be hard to keep multiple targets open, especially for a beginner. After identifying one direction from the deal and the Charleston, you might just want to stay the course. Add in the strategy of multiple hand targeting after you've gotten the hang of things.
- The easiest section on the card is the Consecutive Run section. Often, the second or third Consecutive Run hand is the easiest hand to make.
- Never forget that the pairs are the hardest things to make, because you can't expose them and you can't use jokers in them. If your deal and Charleston suggest a hand with one or more pairs, and you don't have the pair(s) by the end of the Charleston, consider going for a different hand.
- If you're making a hand that uses a pair, and you don't have the pair, watch the discards. When two of that tile are dead, you have just one chance left to make the hand. If your hand isn't ready for mah-jongg and that tile goes out, the hand is dead, and you need to switch to another hand.

- When the player at your left discards a tile you don't need, and you have another one, it's a good idea to throw yours immediately. It might force someone's hand. A player who needs that tile may have been letting the first one go unclaimed, but now must call the second one or give up the hand. Making the player call for exposure gives you valuable information about that player's hand.

- When discarding a tile that's the same as the previous tile, it's a good idea to say "Same" rather than the name of the tile. Another player who needs the tile may not be paying attention and may miss an important tile. Another player's disadvantage is an advantage for you.

- Don't bunch your discards together. Experienced players can read your discards and figure out what you're waiting for.

- Don't separate your concealed (racked) tiles into groups, separated by gaps. Experienced players can read the back of gapped hands and figure out how close you are to finishing the hand.

- When an opponent has made two exposures, you can usually figure out what hand she's making. Discarding a tile she needs is risky at this point. Discarding a tile to three exposures is very dangerous. It might be wiser to break up your hand.

- When it becomes obvious that a particular tile or type of tile is not being used by anyone (like when everybody is throwing winds, and one of the winds is fully dead on the discard floor), consider saving some as safe discards for the later dangerous phase of the game. Best to throw hot tiles early and cold tiles later, if your situation permits.

- Be flexible. As you build your hand, be ready to abandon your earlier thinking about how to build it as you see what tiles you're picking and what tiles others are discarding.

Don't Claim Every Tile You Can

Beginners often fall prey to a misperception—that claiming tiles and making exposures is a privilege, a sign of progress. That's not the nature of exposures at all. Mah-Jongg isn't about making exposures that lead to completing the hand. Mah-Jongg is about completing the hand *before* anyone else does. Making exposures is, actually, the heavy price that must be paid for the privilege of using discards to help you complete the hand.

Try to keep your hand concealed as long as you can, especially if your hand has not yet solidified toward a clear target hand. Whenever you make an exposure, you are revealing your deepest secret intentions to the other players. With one exposure, experienced players of the American game can sometimes make educated guesses about what hand you are making. With the second exposure, most experienced players can probably tell which of one or two hands on the card you are making. Depending on the length of the remaining wall and the tiles they are holding, those players could well take drastic steps to stop you from ever completing your hand. So, before someone discards a tile you need, you should already have it firmly in your mind whether or not you actually want to claim it. Experience will teach you when to go for it and when to wait.

Of course, you shouldn't make any melds if the hand you're working on is marked "C" on the card.

Joker Strategy

- Don't forget that jokers can be redeemed. That's a double-edged sword. If you make a joker exposure, somebody else might be able to get the joker.
- It isn't always a good idea to redeem a joker. If your hand is a Singles And Pairs hand, you don't need jokers. And it's not a good idea to make another player jokerless. If she wins, you have to pay her double. On the other hand, if you discard a redeemable tile, others may suspect that you're doing a Singles And Pairs hand.
- If someone discards a joker or a redeemable tile, that's a clue that she may be working on a Singles And Pairs hand. Or she might be making a hand that contains one or more pairs, and she has all her pungs and kongs (and is waiting to complete a pair).
- Here's a trick, called "Joker Bait," that sometimes can be used to obtain a joker. It often happens that, after the Charleston and after some picking, your hand contains an unwanted pair of tiles. Don't

be too quick to break up the pair. If you can, save the pair until half the wall is left (about the time the last full wall has been served). Throw out the first tile of the pair. If you are lucky, someone will call it and make a joker exposure. Then, on your turn, you can redeem the remaining tile.

- Jokers are always safe discards, because nobody can use them once discarded. When you determine that your hand is a lost cause, dogging (throwing away your jokers) is a safe move when you just don't want somebody else to win.

- When discarding a joker, it's a good idea to say "Same." Another player might not be paying attention and might not notice that you threw away a joker. She would have perked up her ears if you'd said "Joker," but miss it when you say "Same." She might be accordingly unaware of what you are doing with your hand, and throw a tile you need.

- Remember that if someone's kong exposure has 3 naturals and 1 joker, there's only 1 tile that can be used to redeem it. If you pick that tile, you can take your time to redeem it (nobody else is going to get that joker; it's safely yours). Likewise, if someone has a pung exposure with a joker, and the other natural belonging to that set lies dead on the discard floor.

- When you're in a situation like the above (there is a redeemable joker that's safely yours), don't be in a rush to make the exchange. If the other player wins jokerless before you manage to complete your hand, you'll have to pay her double.

- This last tip is arguably a dirty trick, using a loophole in the official rules. If your last move before declaring mah-jongg is to redeem a joker, the league says that's self-pick (thus everyone pays you double), even if the redeemable tile was not the last-picked tile. So if you have a redeemable tile in your hand, and you could use a joker, and the redeemable joker is safely yours alone, then keep the redeemable tile until the hand is otherwise complete. Then make the exchange for mah-jongg, and everyone has to pay you double. It should be noted that this author disagrees with the National Mah Jongg League permitting such a move.

Don't Let Someone Else Win

As much as you want to go out yourself, sometimes it's wiser to keep anybody else from winning. Sometimes discretion is the better part of greed.

Watch the Discards & the Wall

As it approaches the end, the tension increases. It's more important to be careful what you discard when there are fewer tiles remaining to be drawn. Check the discard floor to see if any of your needed tiles are dead. Check the discard floor and the exposures to see if a tile you are planning to discard might be "hot."

Even tiles that have been discarded before can be "hot" in American mah-jongg. Someone might be holding enough jokers to make a pung or kong without having any naturals in the hand.

ADVANCED STRATEGY

- When your tiles clearly point to one particular hand, go for it without worrying about giving clues about your intentions. Especially if you are ready early, opponents will probably risk discarding tiles you need. "It was a long wall" is a common lament when giving the win to an early winner.
- Don't be afraid to go for the high-scoring hands, when dealt junk and no jokers. You probably wouldn't win with a bad deal anyway—might as well try for the gusto.
- Be mindful of your body language and any clues you may be giving others about how well you may think you are doing: habitual postures, changes in breathing, expression, grunts, groans . . .
- When playing against the same opponents on a regular basis, you have an opportunity to observe their mannerisms and habits. For example, consider the lady who plays calmly most of the time, but when ready for mah-jongg she suddenly fidgets with the wall. Or the lady who suddenly seems in a hurry, reaching for the wall before it's her turn, whenever her hand is ready. Little mannerisms like this can be a giveaway.
- When playing with regular opponents, you can learn about their playing style. Some people tend to make a lot of Wind hands. Some

play only Consecutive Run hands. Some are risk takers. Being aware of your opponents' style is good strategy, as Sun Tzu wrote.

• As soon as an opponent has made an exposure, it's wise to start forming guesses as to what hand(s) she may be making. You can test your hypotheses by discarding tiles she might use, if it's early in the game still.

• Just because an opponent passes up a tile you thought she needed doesn't mean she doesn't really need it. Maybe she doesn't have enough of its mates or jokers yet. Or if it's a tile she needs to complete a pair, maybe she doesn't have all her pungs and kongs yet.

D. Variations

TABLE RULES

It is normal for players who get together regularly to make their own table rules to suit the way they want to play. Your group can come up with any special rule or interpretation you desire, so long as:

a. You all agree.
b. You are prepared to work out solutions to problems that may arise from your special rule or interpretation.
c. You are prepared to drop your special rule or interpretation when joining other tables, or attending a tournament.

When newcomers join your regular game, it's important to begin by informing them about your table rules. When you join someone else's regular game, they might forget to begin by informing you about their table rules, so you should ask. It's bad manners and a bad idea to challenge the appropriateness of someone else's table rules; just adapt and be a good sport.

Although there is no standard, some common table rules used by players of the American game are outlined below.

Hot Tile, Hot Wall, Cold Wall

Some players, out of resentment for having to pay when somebody else gives the winning tile, set up a table rule that either prohibits or penalizes throwing a "hot tile."

Such rules have to define clearly exactly when a tile is to be regarded as hot. These rules usually call a tile hot when the wall gets short. Some table rules kick in when the wall is down to the last few stacks remaining in front of the dealer's rack. Other table rules take effect when there are only eight stacks (or some other specific number of stacks) remaining in the wall. Some tournaments set a penalty for discarding a win to two or more exposures (without regard for the length of the wall).

Two common hot tile table rules kick in when the wall reaches a certain length. "Cold wall" rules prohibit the discarding of a predefined hot tile. "Hot wall" rules penalize a player who discards a predefined hot tile, when this action results in a win. The penalty usually is that the discarder must pay for everyone.

These rules sometimes provide safety exceptions. For example, if it can be shown that the tile being discarded is the fourth of its kind, and its three mates are all dead among discards or exposures, it may be permissible to discard the tile. Special safety exceptions must then be made for flowers, since there are eight of those. When the table rule provides a safety exception and someone wins on a supposedly safe yet hot tile, all players would pay as normal.

If your group wishes to set up a hot tile rule of some kind, you need to work out all the details and exceptions yourself. There is no standard (under the official rules, there are no hot tile rules at all).

The Peek Pass

Some tables permit the player to look at tiles being blind passed during the Charleston. This way you can see what you missed, but you're not permitted to use the tiles after looking at them. Such a move can no longer be referred to as a "blind pass," and it doesn't even make sense to call it "stealing"—thus, it is here referred to as a "peek pass." If you peek at the blind pass during a tournament, you'll be declared dead. Therefore, this table rule is not recommended.

Wall Game Kitty

Some tables provide a pot or kitty to which all players (including the bettor, if present) contribute when a wall game occurs (when nobody has made a complete mah-jongg hand, and the wall has run out of tiles). These table rules usually award the kitty to either the next person who wins, or the next person who wins a hand worth more than the minimum 25 points.

High Pie, Low Pie—No Pie, No Money

It's usual to play the game with a $5 pie. Some groups want to limit their risk and play with a lower amount (like $2 or $3), or to play for points only. Some groups want to increase the excitement by raising the pie amount to $10, or playing "with the roof off" (without any pie limit).

Double Dice, Daily Double

Some groups find it interesting to double the stakes only occasionally, as determined by the roll of the dice.

Under the Double Dice table rule, the doubling occurs only when double dice are rolled (two ones, two sixes, etc.). The winner of the hand that begins with double dice will collect double value of her hand. If it's a wall game and a kitty is in use, all players contribute double to the kitty.

Under the Daily Double table rule, the number rolled to begin the evening's play sets the number that will cause a double-score hand to be played. For example, when the hostess's first dice roll of the evening is a 7, then every time a 7 is rolled, that game will score double for the winner.

No Dice

Some groups play without using any dice at all. This table rule is actually a *very bad* idea, because playing without dice makes cheating possible. Under the No Dice table rule, dealer always takes the first four tiles at the right end of her rack (there will be no last remaining portion of a wall in front of the dealer—the end of the wall is always in front of the player to the right of the dealer). When the dealer knows she's going to take the first four tiles at the end of her rack, it's not too difficult for her to palm jokers during the shuffling process, and seed them on her wall. This table rule is most definitely *not* recommended.

Picking Ahead—Future Tile

Many players think that having a faster game is a good thing, and that the game will go faster if each player picks her next tile immediately after discarding (or picking before the player at her left has discarded), without looking at the picked tile until it's her turn.

This practice used to be widespread in the American game in the early days, but it became clear to the NMJL leadership that it was a bad practice because it resulted in too many conflicts when players wanted to call a discard. It was very difficult to call a discard in such a short window, and people often got confused as to the proper way of putting the tiles back on the wall in such cases.

The National Mah Jongg League wrote "No looking ahead" on the card starting in 1947, but that didn't fix the problem. So in 1956 the league wrote "No picking ahead" on the card, and now among the rules on the back of the card is the sentence, in all capital letters: "NO PICKING OR LOOKING AHEAD." It causes too many problems. If your group decides to use a Picking Ahead table rule, you need to work very hard at clearly defining how all possible problem situations are to be resolved. And you cannot expect to get rulings from any outside parties.

One of the biggest problems for players who get used to picking ahead is that it becomes a bad habit. Many a futures players has been called dead at a tournament when her hand automatically went to the wall before her turn. This table rule, too, is most definitely *not* recommended.

Death Declaration Error Penalty

Some tables penalize an erroneous death challenge by making the erring death challenger's hand dead. This sort of rule, however, is difficult to foolproof. When there is a situation in which someone has been called dead by one player, and the other two players can neither confirm nor deny that the challenge is erroneous, then the only way for the challenger to defend herself from also being called dead is to provide details of her reasoning for the challenge. And this kind of discussion is not permissible under the official death rules.

Atomic

Some tables use a rule that awards a special score to a player who makes an "atomic" (or sometimes "bionic" or "nuclear") hand. These tables must define what constitutes an atomic hand (usually seven pairs of anything except jokers), and what circumstances must prevail. Some tables hold that if a player ever gets a joker, the hand is disarmed (no longer atomic). These rules usually stipulate that a player must declare that she's going atomic, and that she must declare when she is no longer atomic. If your group wishes to set up an atomic rule, you have to determine for yourselves all of the foregoing and what the atomic hand will score when won.

East Pays or Receives Double

Some tables may use a rule that doubles the risk and reward for the dealer of each hand. When dealer wins, everyone pays her double. When dealer loses, she pays double. If there is a bettor who bet on the dealer, the bettor shares equally the dealer's doubled risk or doubled reward.

Mish

Some groups seem to enjoy dancing more than others. Two Charlestons and a courtesy aren't enough for these folks, so they permit an additional exchange of tiles. Under this table rule, players place any desired number of unwanted tiles in the middle of the table and "mish" them around. Then everyone takes back the same number of tiles they'd put in.

Frish

Sometimes, after the Charleston, a player may still have such a bad hand that she's permitted to ask for a redeal. If your group wants to set up such a table rule, you have to figure out what to do if someone at the table votes against redealing. Is it a majority vote? Table rules like this are up to you to figure out.

Taking "Same" Tile upon Joker Discard

When discarding jokers, it's the norm to say "Same" or to repeat the name of the previous discard, and when this is done, both the previous discard and the joker are dead. The National Mah Jongg League used to have a rule that permitted players to call for the named tile in such a circumstance (not the joker itself), but that rule was abolished some years ago. Some groups may still play the old way. But it's not recommended.

Reclaiming Discarded Jokers

Some games allow players to use discarded jokers, and it's a race to see who calls for it first. This is probably done more out of ignorance of the official rules than as a table rule that has any merit. It's recommended that the official rules be used instead: once discarded, a joker is dead.

FIVE PLAYERS, SIX PLAYERS—THREE PLAYERS, TWO PLAYERS

More Than Four Players

Many players of the American game enjoy playing with five people. It gives each player a chance to get a break (get a bite to eat, refresh her drink, sit on a different kind of chair for a while, etc.). When rolling the dice to select the dealer, you can use the same results to determine who will sit out the first game. The high roller deals and the low roller sits out. Or perhaps someone will volunteer to sit out the first hand. Or if someone is late, and four of you are ready to begin, the latecomer is automatically the first one to sit out.

There are two ways to play with five players: either the fifth player simply sits out for one hand (every fifth hand), or the fifth player may participate in the game as a silent bettor. If there are six players, the same applies. Two sit out while four play.

I'll Sit This One Out

The fifth player simply relaxes or watches the others as they play. No kibitzing allowed! After the game plays out (either someone wins or it's a wall game), the player who dealt that game gets up from the table, and the fifth player takes that now-vacant seat. If there are six players, one player replaces the former dealer, and the other will be next to take a seat at the table.

Place Your Bets!

When playing with a fifth player as bettor, after the two Charlestons and the "courtesy pass," the bettor examines each player's hand to decide which one she thinks will win.

No talking during viewing time! The bettor must not give any indications to the players as to whose hand is good or whose hand is bad. And it would be unwise for a player to give indications to the bettor as well. In fact, there is even an advantage in not having the bettor know that your hand will prevail—you want the bettor to bet against you so you can collect from her (if you win).

If you are the bettor, you should not only examine each player's tiles to see whose hand is better, but you also need to consider if the players are "in each other's hair," which could make it impossible for someone to win.

Once the bettor has made her decision, she makes a notation of her bet. There are a couple of standard ways to do this: by use of pad and pen or using the plastic device Americans call a "bettor" (a piece not always included with all mah-jongg sets).

Pad and pen: The bettor writes the name of the player who she thinks will win. Or she may write "wall."

Plastic "bettor" device: These items come in a variety of different forms. Originally they were designed to keep track of the "prevailing wind" (a feature of most Asian forms of mah-jongg), but American players have come to use these for betting. If the device shows the letters N, E, W, S on it, then East stands for the dealer, and the other letters stand for the other players. West is the player opposite the dealer, of course. American players tend to regard the player to the right of East as North, and the player to the left of East as South (as if the table were a map). If the device shows the numbers 1, 2, 3, 4 on it, then the 1 stands for the dealer, and the other numbers stand for the other players in counterclockwise order around the table. If the device has a fifth symbol on it, that can be used to bet on a "wall game." The table needs to set its own standard for how to bet on a wall game.

Security: Whether using a plastic bettor or a pad and pen, make sure that the bettor's bet is in a place where the players cannot see the bet. The bet shouldn't be near the refreshments, else players should stay at the table and not go get refreshments until after the bet-on game has been played through to completion. The bet should also be in a place where the bettor cannot go back to it and change her bet once she can see how the game is going.

Play, Already: After the bettor has made her bet, the players at the table play. The bettor must remain silent—no commenting allowed. If the bettor is excited about watching the game play itself out, she should not hover conspicuously by one player.

Once someone has won, the bettor's bet can be checked. When the four seated players agree to pay accordingly, the bettor pays or is paid according to how she bet. If the bet-on player has won, the bettor collects just as the winner did (same amount from each player). If the bet-on player did not win, the bettor must pay exactly the same that the bet-on player did, to any and all players that the bet-on player does.

Errors When Playing with a Bettor

When a player makes an erroneous exposure, the bettor must remain silent. A death challenge, or any observation or comment about the ongoing game, may come only from a sitting player.

FEWER THAN FOUR PLAYERS

Three Players: Build four walls. Deal 13 tiles to each player (14 to the dealer) as normal. Just skip the empty seat (nobody is West, for example)—do not deal tiles to the empty seat; empty seat is never the dealer. Skip the Charleston, just go straight to the dealer's first discard.

Some people reject the idea of skipping the Charleston, and make a table rule governing how to do a Charleston with three players. For example, one way to do a three-handed Charleston is as follows.

- Pass to, and take from, all four seats.
- When passing to the empty seat, place the three tiles by the wall at that side of the table.

- When taking tiles from the empty seat, take any three tiles from the wall at that side of the table.
- At the end of the Charleston, the wall on the empty side of the table must be repaired prior to play.

Two Players: Same. Sit opposite each other. Build four walls. Dealer has 14 tiles, opposite player has 13 tiles (as usual). No Charleston. No dummy seats.

One Player: There are some solitaire computer games that are played with mah-jongg tiles. You can obtain these games on the Internet (see Appendix). The benefit of a solitaire game is that it helps the player become adept at spotting tiles among the discards and exposures atop the racks of other players.

4

CHINESE OFFICIAL MAHJONG

The official Chinese rules were first codified in 1998, in order to create a legal, nongambling set of rules under which the game of mahjong could be played in China. The official Chinese rules have been known by a variety of names, depending on the translation or the source. They may be referred to as Chinese Official (CO), or Official International Rules (OIR), or Chinese Mahjong Contest Rules (CMCR), or World Mahjong Contest Rules (WMCR). The most recent rule book published at the time of this writing is entitled simply *Mahjong Competition Rules*.

The body in charge of publishing the rules and sanctioning official competitions has been known by a variety of names as well: the Organization of the World Mahjong Contest Center, or the World Mahjong Contest Committee. The most recent name at the time of this writing is World Mahjong Organization (WMO).

The official Chinese rules are subject to updates and improvements by the WMO. The detailed rules are available in English, and it's recommended that the reader obtain those rules for a thorough understanding of all the rules as they evolve. This book introduces the reader to the basics of the official game, and offers strategy tips above and beyond the rules themselves.

In the latest rule book, the WMO refers to the game by the spelling "mahjong" (as one word, no hyphen, and with one G). That spelling is used throughout this chapter.

Distinguishing Characteristics of Chinese Official Mahjong

The official Chinese game is a pattern-based Asian game, in which the usual hand structure is "four sets and a pair," in which a set may be a chow, a pung, or a kong. Unlike the American game, which is kept fresh by issuing a new list of allowed hands every year, Asian variants endure because of the rich possibilities of a nearly infinite number of combinations.

Particularly, the chow gives Asian variants their depth and longevity. A chow is a numerical sequence of three suit tiles.

Two example chows: a 123 of Craks, and a 678 of Bams.

The use of chows increases the possibilities and enriches the potential for interesting patterns, keeping the game fresh without having to make yearly changes.

Flowers are not used in the hand to form sets. In Asian forms of mahjong, flowers are tiles that can increase the score if the player wins. There are no jokers.

The official Chinese game is further characterized by the 81 *fan* (scoring elements) and a simple additive scoring system, involving no multiplication or doubling whatsoever.

Unlike all other forms of mahjong, the official Chinese rules involve no money payments between players. The rules were intended for use in competitions, and have been used already for tournaments in China, Japan, and Europe.

A. Rules of Chinese Official Mahjong

This is a detailed statement of the rules, without illustration. A more explanatory description of how to set up and play, with illustrations and examples, is given in Section B of this chapter. This section is good to bookmark or photocopy for novice players, or to answer sticky questions.

Chinese Official mahjong, properly called World Mahjong Competition Rules mahjong, is governed by the World Mahjong Organization (also known as the World Majiang Competition Committee). The rules stated here are based on the rules as publicly defined by the WMO as of early 2007. The WMO may issue changes to these rules at any time. If any difference is found between the rules stated here and rules as stated by the WMO (either in the original Chinese-language rule book or Web site, or in any new book or Web site issued by the WMO), the WMO rules hold sway.

THE TILES

1. The game is played using a standard 144-tile Asian set, without jokers.
2. The 144-tile Asian set consists of suit tiles, honor tiles, and flower tiles.
3. The three suits, called Dots, Bams, and Craks, consist of tiles numbered from 1 to 9, each number quadruplicated within the suit. Thus, there are 36 tiles per suit, for a total of 108 suit tiles.
4. The honor tiles consist of 4 different wind tiles, E, S, W, and N, each quadruplicated, and 3 different dragon tiles, white, green, and red, each quadruplicated. Thus, there are 16 wind tiles and 12 dragon tiles.
5. The 8 flower tiles typically are decorated with images of flowers, and consist of 4 tiles marked in Chinese with flower names and 4 tiles marked with season names, but may instead be decorated with images of people, animals, buildings, vehicles, or objects, and marked with Chinese characters that tell a story. Flower tiles may be marked with numbers. The images, markings, and numbers on flower tiles have no significance in this game. They are all simply called "flower" (in Chinese, *hua*, pronounced *hwar*).

THE TABLE, THE HALL, & THE PLAYERS

6. The game is played by four persons, each one competing against the other three, not partnered. Collusion between players is forbidden.

7. The game requires a table, no smaller than 33 inches (83 centimeters) square and no larger than 36 inches (91 centimeters) square. There must be four chairs suitable for the table.

8. There must be a pair of cubical dice, for use in randomly selecting the place where the wall shall be broken, so as to prevent cheating.

9. Score may be kept on paper or with chips. If chips are used, final scores must be recorded on score sheets and turned in to the judges.

10. Tables are arrayed in the competition hall with sufficient space between tables, and aisles for movement.

11. The eastern wall of the hall is marked with a sign bearing the Chinese character meaning "east." Other walls may be marked according to their associated winds, or with the Chinese characters for "quiet" and "merit."

12. Players are assigned to a table by the competition's organizing committee.

13. The first dealer ("East") may be selected by the following procedure (details may vary).

    a. Players sit in any chair to begin the procedure.

    b. Four wind tiles (one of each wind) are mixed facedown and stacked or arrayed in a line.

    c. A player is selected to take the first tile. Selection may occur by rolling dice (high roller takes first tile) or an honored visitor may take the first tile.

    d. Other players, continuing counterclockwise around the table, take a tile.

    e. The tiles are turned faceup and examined. Each tile represents a seat at the table. Players go to their respective seats. South sits to the right of East; North sits to the left of East.

THE DEAL

14. The players shuffle the tiles facedown, then each player builds a wall, two tiles high and eighteen stacks long. Each player's wall is pushed in toward the other players' walls, forming a "great wall" in the shape of a square.

15. East (also called "dealer") rolls two dice to determine which player shall roll the dice a second time. Count from the dealer counterclockwise around the table.
    a. 2, 6, and 10 indicate the player at dealer's right (South).
    b. 3, 7, and 11 indicate the player opposite the dealer (West).
    c. 4, 8, and 12 indicate the player at dealer's left (North).
    d. 5 and 9 indicate the dealer himself.
16. Player indicated by the dice ("second roller") rolls the two dice a second time to determine where the wall is to be broken.
    a. The number rolled by the dealer is added to the number shown by the second roll of the dice.
    b. The resulting number indicates the number of stacks to be counted before breaking the wall.
        i.   If the number is lower than 18, the break is within the second roller's wall. The break is made after counting the indicated number of stacks, so that the number of stacks to the right of the break is the total number resulting from the two rolls of the dice.
        ii. If the number is higher than 18, the break is in the wall to the left of the second roller.
        iii. If the number is 18, the deal commences with the right end of wall to the left of the second roller (the "break" is between the walls).
17. The dealer himself takes 4 tiles (two stacks) after (counterclockwise from) the break in the wall, and places them in front of himself.
18. South (the player at dealer's right, counterclockwise from the dealer) takes the next 4 tiles (two stacks) continuing clockwise from the break in the wall. Each player, taking turns counterclockwise around the table, takes 4 tiles (two stacks) continuing clockwise around the wall, until each player has taken thrice (is holding 12 tiles).
19. The dealer now takes the top tile from the first stack on the end of the wall, and the top tile from the third stack from the end of the wall, so that he is now holding 14 tiles.
20. Each nondealer player, taking turns counterclockwise around the

table, now takes 1 tile from the end of the wall (the player to dealer's right taking the end tile, then the player opposite the dealer taking the top tile, then the player to the dealer's left taking the end tile). Each player who is not the dealer is now holding 13 tiles.

21. Each player may now examine his tiles, standing them on end in a straight line in front of himself so that he can see the tiles but no other player can see them. He may organize his tiles by number, suit, and type in any fashion that helps him strategize the hand about to be played.

THE OBJECT OF THE GAME

22. The object of the game is to form a complete hand before anyone else does.

23. A complete hand may be structured in one of the permissible ways, as follows:
    a. Four sets and a pair, in which the term "set" is used to mean a chow, pung, or kong, which are defined as follows:
       i. A chow is a set composed of 3 sequentially numbered suit tiles of the same suit;
       ii. A pung is a set composed of 3 identical nonflower tiles;
       iii. A kong is a set composed of 4 identical nonflower tiles;
       iv. A pair is composed of 2 identical nonflower tiles;
    b. Seven pairs;
    c. Thirteen single honors and terminals plus a duplicate of any;
    d. Fourteen single unconnected tiles (the special hands of the knitted category).

24. The hand must be worth a minimum of eight (8) points, excluding points for flower tiles.

REPLACING FLOWER TILES

25. Flower tiles are not used in the hand. Rather, they are melded and replaced. After a hand has been won, the player who won earns extra points for melded flowers.

26. After the deal, East (dealer) announces how many flowers, if any, he is holding.

27. Saying "*Hwar*" as he takes a replacement tile from the back end of the wall (the opposite end from that used during the deal and

used during play), he examines each new tile to see if it is a flower or not. He takes as many replacement tiles as needed so that his standing concealed flowerless tiles number 14.

28. Once the dealer's hand contains no concealed flowers, the dealer customarily gestures to South (the player at the dealer's right).

29. Each player in turn, counterclockwise around the table, takes replacements for any flowers, examining the replacements to determine if any are flowers, until each player is holding 13 standing concealed flowerless tiles.

30. When a player has no flowers, it is customary to say so when it's that player's turn to replace flowers.

31. When all players have replaced flowers, the game may begin.

32. When during the course of play, a player picks a flower, he may expose the flower and take a replacement tile.

33. It is permissible instead to discard a flower rather than take a replacement; this is usually done as a defensive measure later in the play when discarding becomes dangerous. A flower that was discarded, not melded, does not earn points.

PLAY

34. The dealer, provided he is unable to declare mahjong, begins the game by discarding a tile.

35. The dealer's first discard must occur within 20 seconds of flower replacement.

36. When discarding, the player must silently place the tile in an orderly fashion on the discard floor.

    a. Discards are placed in neat rows, left to right, in front of each player, between the center of the table and the player's hand, leaving room to meld exposures between the discards and the player's hand.

    b. Each row should be six tiles long.

    c. Subsequent rows are placed beneath previous rows (nearer the player).

37. Normally, each player in turn, counterclockwise from the dealer, picks a tile from the wall (the same end of the wall used during the deal), bringing the tile total (not counting flowers or the fourth tile in a kong) to 14, then discards a tile, returning his

hand's tile total (not counting flowers or the fourth tile in a kong) to 13. Discarding must occur within 10 seconds from the time the player acquired the fourteenth tile.

38. This order of play may be thought of as flowing downhill; the player at one's right is called the "lower" seat; the player at one's left is called the "upper" seat.

39. An alternate way to acquire one's fourteenth tile is by taking a discard.

    a. The most recently discarded tile is available for another player to call;

    b. The tile may be called to complete a set, or to declare mahjong;

    c. All previously discarded tiles are "covered" by the most recent discard, and are regarded as dead tiles.

CLAIMING A DISCARD FOR A MELDED SET

40. A player may claim the current live discard to make an exposure, provided that certain prerequisites are met:

    a. The call must be made within 3 seconds of the time the tile was discarded (the "window of opportunity");

    b. The player must have enough other tiles to form a complete set;

    c. The set being completed may be only a chow, a pung, or a kong (not a pair and not a knitted set);

    d. The set completed by the discarded tile must be exposed to the view of the other players;

    e. A chow may be completed and melded with a tile discarded by the player at the claimant's left (the player's "upper seat") *only*; a chow may never be completed and melded with a tile discarded by the players opposite the claimant or to the claimant's right. Because of this, each player is said to "feed" chowable tiles to his lower seat.

41. To claim a discard, the player must vocalize the claim.

    a. The player must say *"Peng"* (pronounced "pung") to claim a discard to complete and meld a pung;

    b. The player must say "Kong" or *"Gang"* to claim a discard to complete and meld a kong;

    c. The player must say "Chow" or "*Chur*" or "*Chi*" to claim a discard from the player at the left to complete and meld a chow;

    d. The player must speak the claim loudly and clearly enough that all players can hear the claim.

42. After vocalizing the claim for the discard, the player should expose the tiles of the set being completed, take the claimed discard, and form the completed set.

    a. The meld should be placed between the player's standing tiles and the player's discards (between the standing tiles and the wall, if present).

    b. The taken tile should be rotated 90 degrees so that all players can see which tile had been a discard;

    c. The rotated taken tile should be placed among the other tiles of the set so as to indicate which player had discarded it;

        i. If discarded by the player at one's right, the rotated taken tile is placed to the right of the other tiles of the set;

        ii. If discarded by the opposite player, the rotated taken tile is placed in the middle of the other tiles of the set;

        iii. If discarded by the player at one's left, the rotated taken tile is placed to the left of the other tiles of the set, even if the set is a chow and this results in the tiles being displayed in nonsequential order.

43. After claiming a discard and melding a kong, the player must take a replacement tile from the back end of the wall (the opposite end of the wall from the end used to take tiles normally).

44. The player shall then discard, completing his turn.

45. After a player has melded a set and discarded, the order of play continues counterclockwise from he who melded (not from he who discarded). In the case of a chow, no interruption in the order of play occurs.

CONCEALED KONGS

46. When a player, through the deal or through picking, comes into possession of a completed set concealed in the hand, it is neither necessary nor permissible to meld the set, with the exception of the kong.

47. When a player is building a normal "four sets and a pair" hand, and a set is composed of 4 identical tiles, it becomes impossible to complete the hand with 14 tiles. Thus, the player is permitted to meld the set and take a replacement tile.

48. The player shall put his 4 identical tiles facedown (still concealed) in his melds area (between the standing tiles and the discards) and say "Kong," then take a replacement tile from the back end of the wall.

49. For scoring purposes, a melded concealed kong is not regarded to be exposed (a hand that includes melded concealed kongs and no exposed melds is regarded to be concealed, and may earn points for concealment).

KONG PROMOTION

50. An exposed pung may be promoted to a kong only when the player self-picks the fourth tile (a discard may not be taken for this purpose).

TWO PLAYERS CLAIM SAME DISCARD

51. When two players claim the same discarded tile, the tile doesn't necessarily go to the player who spoke first. Provided that both claims are spoken within a reasonably short time, conflicting claims are resolved as follows:

    a. When one player claims a discarded tile for chow and the other claims it for pung, the pung call trumps the chow call.

    b. When two players claim a discarded tile, one to complete a set and one for mahjong, the mahjong call trumps the exposure call.

    c. When two players claim a discarded tile for mahjong, the player nearest in turn to the discarder gets the tile.

CLAIMING A DISCARD FOR A WIN

52. Any player may claim the current live discard for mahjong at any time, (i) regardless of whose turn it is and (ii) regardless of the size of the set completed by the discard.

53. To claim a discard for mahjong, the player must vocalize the claim.

   a. The player must say *"Hu."* It is properly said in a low rising tone (without sounding quizzical).

   b. The player must speak the claim loudly and clearly enough that all players can hear the claim.

   c. The player must speak the claim while the window of opportunity is open (before 3 seconds have passed).

54. After vocalizing the claim for mahjong, the player must expose all his tiles and take the discard to complete the hand.

   a. The concealed standing tiles must be laid flat, faceup, for all to see. Tiles of a concealed kong need to be revealed as well.

   b. It is forbidden to take the discard and put it in the hand, burying it among the tiles of the hand, subject to the penalty of "death." See "Errors & Penalties," (page 142). The winning tile must be placed apart or rotated or stacked; some clear indication that this is the final tile taken.

   c. The winner is required to identify the winning hand to the satisfaction of the other players. The winner must enumerate all *fan* and their associated points, and the hand must earn no less than 8 points.

   d. Scoring is displayed to other players using the winner's discarded tiles, as described in "Scoring & Payment," (page 138).

   e. Performing the above steps out of order may be grounds for a penalty; see "Errors & Penalties," (page 142).

55. The other players should not expose their hands prior to confirmation of the winning hand.

WINNING BY SELF-PICK

56. A player who picks a tile that completes his hand must announce the fact to the other players.

   a. The player must say *"Hu."* It is properly said in a low rising tone (without sounding quizzical).

   b. The player must speak the claim loudly and clearly enough that all players can hear the claim.

57. After speaking, the winner must then display the hand.
    a. The concealed standing tiles must be laid flat, faceup, for all to see. Tiles of a concealed kong must be revealed as well.
    b. The winning tile must be placed apart, or rotated, or stacked; some clear indication that this is the final tile picked, especially if the winning tile fulfills Single Wait, Edge Wait, or Closed Wait, or other *fan* requiring a special waiting state (such as Nine Gates).
    c. The winner is required to identify the winning hand to the satisfaction of the other players. The winner must enumerate all *fan* and their associated points.
    d. The hand must earn no less than 8 points, before flower points are added.
    e. Scoring is displayed to other players using the winner's discarded tiles, as described in "Scoring & Payment," below.
    f. Performing the above steps out of order may be grounds for a penalty; see "Errors & Penalties," (page 142).
58. The other players should not expose their hands prior to confirmation of the winning hand.

NOBODY WINS

59. If all wall tiles are taken without anyone declaring *"Hu,"* each player scores 0 points for the hand. The deal moves to the next player counterclockwise from the previous dealer.
60. If the last tile taken from the wall is used to make a kong, the konging player needn't discard a tile.

SCORING & PAYMENT

61. In an international tournament, not all players speak the same language. To facilitate communication during scoring, tiles from the winner's discards are used to visually indicate the points earned;
    a. A single faceup tile represents 1 point;
    b. A single facedown tile represents 10 points.
    c. The player must not use any of the tiles of his hand for this display; see "Errors & Penalties," (page 142).
62. The player is permitted to add the points for multiple *fan* em-

bodied by the winning hand, except as otherwise indicated in "The *Fan* & Their Respective Values," (page 146), that are subject to the five scoring principles in 64.

63. The player shall identify the primary scoring element first, then add other scoring elements that are not inevitably related to, or derived from, the primary scoring element or by one another.

64. In calculating the hand's score, the following principles must be observed.

   a. **Prohibition Against Implied Inclusions:** When a high-scoring pattern cannot be made without also making a lesser pattern, the lesser pattern is said to be "implied," and may not also be scored.

   b. **Prohibition Against Separation:** Once some sets have been combined to create a particular scoring element, the player may not "separate" the tiles of those sets and reorganize them into other sets to form a different scoring element.

   c. **Prohibition Against Identical Patterns:** Once a set has been used to form a particular two- or three-set pattern, the player may not use the same set to form an identical pattern with another set.

   d. **Freedom of Choice Principle:** If a set can be used to form a low-scoring pattern or a high-scoring pattern, and both cannot be scored, the player is free to claim the higher-scoring pattern.

   e. **Prohibition Against Repetitive Set Usage:** Once two or three sets have been combined for a scoring pattern, any other remaining sets in the hand may be combined only once with an already-scored set, when creating additional two- or three-set scoring patterns.

65. The winner is required to inform all other players how much each player must pay.

   a. The winner is not permitted to claim more points than other players recognize and validate.

   b. No other player should assist the winner in adding his score. If the winner claims fewer points than he could, other players remain silent.

c. If the winner cannot add the score but other players recognize that it is worth at least 8 points, the player scores only 8 points.

66. The total arrived by adding together all permissible *fan* is called the "basic score."

67. Eight "extra points" are added to the basic score to arrive at the amount each player pays the winner, as follows:
   a. When won by discard, the discarder pays the winner the basic score plus 8 extra points.
   b. When won by discard, the two nondiscarding players pay the winner 8 points only.
   c. When won by self-pick, all nonwinners pay the winner the basic score plus 8 extra points.

68. Penalty points, if any, are also added or deducted as appropriate.

69. Typically, score is kept on a score sheet with a pen. Points are added and subtracted mathematically. Negative scores are possible when scoring on paper.

70. Score may also be kept by means of chips or sticks. To avoid the problem of negative scores, each player should begin the game with 500 points when scoring with chips or sticks. At the end of the game, players' scores are recorded on the score sheet.

71. In a tournament, each player is awarded "table points" according to his total score for a game session as follows:
   a. High scorer earns 4 table points.
   b. Second highest scorer earns 2 table points.
   c. Second lowest scorer earns 1 table point.
   d. Lowest scorer earns 0 table points.
   e. If two players' scores are equal, they split table points between them.
   f. There being a total of 7 table points to go around, tied high scorers both earn 3 table points, second highest scorer earns 1 table point, and the remaining two earn 0 table points (3-3-1-0 rather than 4-2-1-0).

72. At the end of the game, each player signs his score and the score sheets are delivered to the tournament scorekeeper.

73. At the end of a tournament, players are ranked according to their

total table scores. Players with equal table scores are ranked according to their total cumulative scores ("contest points"). Players with equal table scores and equal total cumulative contest scores are tied for the same rank.

GAME STRUCTURE

74. A complete game (in Chinese: *ju*) is composed of sixteen hands (*pan*) divided into four rounds (*quan*) of four hands each.
    a. One hand is that portion of a game preceded by the building of the walls and ended in one of two ways:
       i. Someone declares "*Hu*," or:
       ii. The tiles of the wall are depleted without anyone declaring *hu*.
    b. After a hand has been played, the dice move to the next counterclockwise player. The player who rolls the dice is called "dealer" and is also called "East." Only the first dealer and the first dealer of each subsequent round actually sit in the easternmost seat.
    c. Each time the dice return to the easternmost seat, a new round begins. In each round four hands are played, with each player acting as dealer once.
    d. The rounds are named for the four winds, in the order East, South, West, and North.
    e. When all four rounds have been played, the game ends.
    f. In a tournament, there may be a time limit imposed for each game. In such an event, the game ends when the time limit runs out or four rounds are played, whichever happens first.

SEAT ROTATION

75. At the end of each round (*quan*) the players stand and change seats.
    a. At the beginning of the South round, East and South exchange seats; North and West exchange seats.
    b. At the beginning of the West round, East and South move to the opposite seats; North moves to the East seat; West moves to the South seat.

    c. At the beginning of the North round, East and South exchange seats; North and West exchange seats.

    d. To look at the rotation throughout the four rounds another way:

        i. Original East moves E, S, N, W (right, across, left).

        ii. Original South moves S, E, W, N (left, across, right).

        iii. Original West moves W, N, E, S (clockwise around the table).

        iv. Original North moves N, W, S, E (counterclockwise around the table).

ERRORS & PENALTIES

76. Penalties may be imposed for errors, rule violations, disruptive behavior, cheating, deriving illegal benefit from the game, or other misconduct.

77. In increasing order of severity, penalties are as follows:

    a. Warning;

    b. Forced discard of a tile;

    c. Loss of basic points;

    d. Prohibition against declaring mahjong; player continues to play but is forbidden to win ("death");

    e. Loss of competitive rank;

    f. Disqualification from present and/or future tournaments.

78. Erroneous exposure (making a meld with mismatched tiles, or failing to take the claimed discard within two turns) invalidates the hand; the player is prohibited from declaring mahjong in the current hand.

79. Empty calling (changing one's mind about taking a discard for exposure) is penalized first by a warning; each repeat violation is subject to increasing loss of points as follows:

    a. Second occurrence: 5 points;

    b. Third occurrence: 10 points;

    c. Fourth occurrence: 20 points;

    d. And doubling for each repeat occurrence.

80. Touching the wall tile before one's upper seat has discarded is penalized first by a warning; the second occurrence is penal-

ized by loss of 5 points; each subsequent occurrence doubles the penalty.

81. Seeing or revealing the wall tile before one's upper seat has discarded is penalized by disqualification from declaring mahjong for the duration of the current hand.

82. Reaching toward the wall commits the player to picking a tile from the wall; he may not change his mind and take the current live discard instead. Doing so is penalized by prohibition from making further exposures and from declaring mahjong for the duration of the current hand.

83. Declaring pung more than 3 seconds after a tile was discarded ("late pung call") is penalized first by a warning; the second occurrence is penalized by loss of 5 points; each subsequent occurrence doubles the penalty.

84. Different ways a player can err in declaring mahjong (*hu*) are penalized as follows:

    a. Declaring mahjong erroneously with a valid ready hand is penalized by loss of 10 points to each of the other players and prohibition from declaring *hu* for the duration of the current hand.

    b. Declaring mahjong erroneously with an unready hand (calling while the hand is waiting for 2 tiles rather than 1, or has a wrong tile count, for example) is penalized by loss of 20 points to each of the other players and prohibition from declaring *hu* for the duration of the current hand.

    c. Making an "empty *hu*" (saying "*Hu*" but not exposing the hand) is penalized by prohibition from declaring *hu* for the duration of the current hand (no penalty points are applied).

    d. Taking the called discard (the winning tile) *after* beginning to count the score invalidates the win and is penalized by prohibition from declaring *hu* for the duration of the current hand, and the player pays 10 points to each opponent.

    e. Saying "Chow" or "Pung" or "Kong" and then changing the call to "*Hu*" is not permitted. The player must make the chow or pung or kong, then discard a tile. (The player is permitted to win subsequently, if possible.)

f. Showing all one's tiles without first saying *"Hu"* invalidates the win; the player pays 10 points to each player and is penalized by prohibition from declaring *hu* for the duration of the current hand.

g. Using tiles from the hand to display the hand's score (when only discards are supposed to be used for this purpose) invalidates the win; the player pays 10 points to each player and is prohibited from declaring *hu* for the duration of the current hand.

h. Making a hand worth less than 8 points invalidates the win; the player pays 10 points to each player and is prohibited from declaring *hu* for the duration of the current hand.

85. Different ways a player can err by exposing tiles are penalized as follows:

a. When a player reveals one of his own tiles, he must discard it on his next turn.

b. When a player reveals all of his own tiles after another player declares mahjong but before the other player's hand is verified, and the win is determined to be valid, the player is penalized by a warning.

c. When a player reveals all of his own tiles after another player declares mahjong but before the other player's hand is verified, and the win is determined to be invalid, the player is penalized by loss of 10 points to each other player, is prohibited from declaring *hu* for the duration of the current hand, and must discard his revealed tiles one by one until all are discarded.

d. A player who reveals his tiles while erroneously declaring mahjong is penalized only for the erroneous *hu* declaration; he is not also penalized for erroneously exposing tiles. He may continue playing normally, without having to discard all his tiles, but may not win.

e. A player who reveals an opponent's tiles is penalized 5 points per revealed tile, paid to the opponent. The referee may also impose a prohibition from declaring *hu*.

86. A player whose hand contains the wrong number of tiles is pe-

nalized by prohibition from declaring *hu* for the duration of the current hand.

87. A player who overtly gives information to another player by any means is penalized by prohibition from declaring *hu* for the duration of the current hand, regardless of whether or not the other player gains benefit from the information.

88. In a tournament, arriving to the table late incurs a penalty depending on the degree of lateness, as follows:
    a. When the player is late by 10 minutes or less, the penalty is 10 points;
    b. When the player is late by more than 10 minutes and up to and including 15 minutes, the penalty is 20 points;
    c. When the player is late by more than 15 minutes, the player forfeits the game, earning 0 table points for the game session.

89. A player who disturbs the competition and/or disobeys the judges may be disqualified from the competition, and may be openly reprimanded.

90. Not taking a called discard until after two turns have passed is penalized by prohibition from declaring *hu* for the duration of the current hand.

91. An incorrect melded set (for example, using a flower as a One Bam) must be left as is, and the player may not declare *hu* for the duration of the current hand.

92. An incorrect flower meld (for example, mistaking a One Bam for a flower) may be claimed for *hu* by another player if the tile is the last of its kind (Last Tile is awarded).

93. A player is not permitted to ask for rulings on events that occurred in the past; the player must request the ruling at the time the event occurs.

APPEALS

94. A player or his team leader may submit an appeal to a referee's judgment.
    a. The appeal must be submitted within 30 minutes of the judgment;
    b. The appeal must be submitted in writing;

    c. The appeal must be signed by the player and/or his team leader;

    d. An appeal fee of U.S. $200 in cash must accompany the submission of the appeal;

        i. If the appeal is upheld, the fee is returned to the complainant;

        ii. If the appeal is denied, the fee is forfeited.

THE *FAN* & THEIR RESPECTIVE VALUES

95. There are 81 scoring elements (*fan*), as follows:

1. Big Four Winds
    a. Value: 88 points.
    b. Pungs or kongs of all four of the winds.
    c. May not combine with Big Three Winds, Little Four Winds, All Pungs, Seat Wind, Prevalent Wind, or Pung of Terminals or Honors.

2. Big Three Dragons
    a. Value: 88 points.
    b. Pungs or kongs of all three of the dragons.
    c. May not combine with Dragon Pungs or Two Dragons.

3. All Green
    a. Value: 88 points.
    b. Tiles are all green. The only tiles that can be used in this hand (in any combination) are the 2, 3, 4, 6, or 8 of Bams and the Green Dragon.
    c. When combined with Seven Pairs, Tile Hog may not be added. May combine with Half Flush or Full Flush.

4. Nine Gates
    a. Value: 88 points.
    b. Tiles of one suit only, with concealed pungs of both terminals (1's and 9's) and 1 of each simple, and (as the final winning tile) a duplicate of any tile in the hand. Prior to obtaining the final tile, the hand was concealed, waiting for any tile in the suit to win (a nine-way wait).
    c. May not be combined with Full Flush (implied), Concealed, Edge Wait, Closed Wait, Single Wait, or Pung of Terminals or Honors. If self-picked, Fully Concealed may be added.

5. Four Kongs

a. Value: 88 points.

b. A hand made with 4 kongs, regardless how many are concealed or exposed (points for concealment may be added).

c. May not be combined with Single Wait.

6. Seven Shifted Pairs

a. Value: 88 points.

b. Tiles of one suit only, forming seven sequentially numbered pairs.

c. May not combine with Full Flush, Concealed Hand, or Single Wait. If self-picked, Fully Concealed may be added.

7. Thirteen Orphans

a. Value: 88 points.

b. Hand consists of one of each terminal and honor, plus a duplicate of any.

c. Points for All Types, Concealed Hand, or Single Wait may not be added. If self-picked, Fully Concealed may be added.

8. All Terminals

a. Value: 64 points.

b. Hand consists solely of 1's and 9's.

c. May not be combined with All Pungs, Outside Hand, or No Honors. Double Pung and Triple Pung may be combined. When combined with Seven Pairs, Tile Hog may not be added.

9. Little Four Winds

a. Value: 64 points.

b. Pungs of three winds, and a pair of the fourth.

c. May combine with Seat Wind and Prevalent Wind, but not with Big Three Winds or Pung of Terminals or Honors.

10. Little Three Dragons

a. Value: 64 points.

b. Pungs or kongs of two dragons, and a pair of the third.

c. May not combine with Dragon Pung or Two Dragons.

11. All Honors

a. Value: 64 points.

b. Pairs, pungs, or kongs of winds and dragons only.

    c. May not combine with All Pungs, Outside Hand, or Pung of Terminals or Honors. Points for Dragon Pung, Prevalent Wind, Seat Wind may be added.

12. Four Concealed Pungs

    a. Value: 64 points.

    b. Four pungs, all made the hard way (without melding).

    c. May not combine with Concealed Hand or All Pungs. If self-picked, Fully Concealed may be added.

13. Pure Terminal Chows

    a. Value: 64 points.

    b. Two 1-2-3 chows and two 7-8-9 chows, and a pair of 5's, all in the same suit.

    c. May not combine with Full Flush, All Chows, Seven Pairs, Pure Double Chow, Mixed Double Chow, or Two Terminal Chows.

14. Quadruple Chow

    a. Value: 48 points.

    b. Four identical chows (same numerical sequence, same suit).

    c. May not combine with Tile Hog, Pure Triple Chow, Pure Double Chow, or Pure Shifted Pungs.

15. Four Pure Shifted Pungs

    a. Value: 48 points.

    b. Four pungs in one suit, each shifted up one number from the last.

    c. May not combine with All Pungs or Pure Triple Chow.

16. Four Shifted Chows

    a. Value: 32 points.

    b. Four chows in one suit, all shifted up one number from the last, or all shifted up two numbers from the last.

    c. May not combine with Short Straight.

17. Three Kongs

    a. Value: 32 points.

    b. A hand with 3 kongs.

    c. Points for concealment may be added; if all 3 kongs are concealed, Three Concealed Pungs may be combined.

18. All Terminals and Honors
a. Value: 32 points.
b. Pairs, pungs, or kongs of terminals, winds, and/or dragons only.
c. May not combine with All Pungs, Outside Hand, or Pung of Terminals or Honors.

19. Seven Pairs
a. Value: 24 points.
b. Seven pairs of any tiles.
c. May not combine with Concealed Hand or Single Wait. May combine with All Types and Tile Hog. If self-picked, Fully Concealed may be added.

20. Greater Honors and Knitted Tiles
a. Value: 24 points.
b. One of each dragon and wind, plus any 7 tiles of an incomplete knitted straight. (A knitted straight is 1-4-7 in one suit, 2-5-8 in another suit, and 3-6-9 in the third suit.)
c. May not combine with Concealed Hand or All Types.

21. All Even Pungs
a. Value: 24 points.
b. A hand formed with four pungs and a pair of even-numbered suit tiles.
c. May not combine with All Pungs or All Simples.

22. Full Flush ("Pure")
a. Value: 24 points.
b. A hand using tiles of one suit only.
c. May not combine with No Honors.

23. Pure Triple Chow
a. Value: 24 points.
b. Three identical chows.
c. May not combine with Pure Shifted Pungs or Pure Double Chow.

24. Pure Shifted Pungs
a. Value: 24 points.
b. Three sequentially numbered pungs in one suit.
c. May not combine with Pure Triple Chow.

25. Upper Tiles
   a. Value: 24 points.
   b. A hand composed entirely of 7's, 8's, and 9's.
   c. May not combine with No Honors.

26. Middle Tiles
   a. Value: 24 points.
   b. A hand composed entirely of 4's, 5's, and 6's.
   c. May not combine with No Honors or All Simples.

27. Lower Tiles
   a. Value: 24 points.
   b. A hand composed entirely of 1's, 2's, and 3's.
   c. May not combine with No Honors.

28. Pure Straight
   a. Value: 16 points.
   b. One through 9 in one suit (three chows, end to end).

29. Three-Suited Terminal Chows
   a. Value: 16 points.
   b. Opposite-end terminal chows (1-2-3 and 7-8-9) in one suit, opposite-end terminal chows in a second suit, and a pair of 5's in the third suit.
   c. May not combine with All Chows, Two Terminal Chows, or Mixed Double Chow.

30. Pure Shifted Chows
   a. Value: 16 points.
   b. Three chows in one suit, each shifted up one number from the last, or each shifted up two numbers from the last.

31. All Fives
   a. Value: 16 points.
   b. Each set (including the pair) includes a 5.
   c. May not combine with All Simples.

32. Triple Pung
   a. Value: 16 points.
   b. Three pungs of the same number in each suit.

33. Three Concealed Pungs
   a. Value: 16 points.
   b. Three pungs made the hard way (without melding).

Chinese money-suited cards.

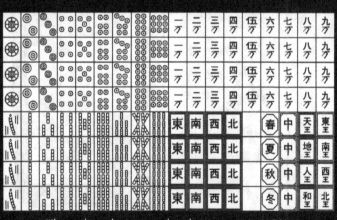

The earliest documented mah-jongg set (c.1873).

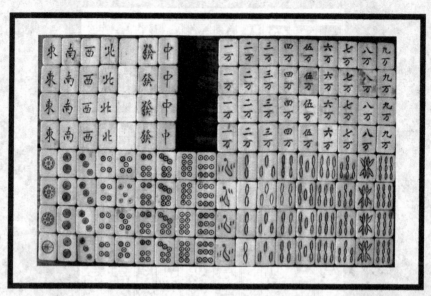

Pre-Babcock tiles, c. 1901 (Qing Dynasty).

Babcock's "red book," softcover (L) and hardcover (R).

Just a few of the many mah-jongg books of the 1920s.

Chinese Majiang Competition Rules (1998)

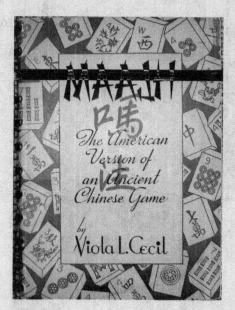

The National Mah Jongg
League made history with its
version in the late 1930s.

The National Mah Jongg League
card alternates colors each year.

NNNNN DDDD 11111 (Quint Any Wind & Any No. In Any Suit, Kong Any Dragon) . . . . **x 40**

Example of color-coding from an American card

NEWS 2007 GGG RRR (Any 2 and 7 Same Suit, Pung Green & Red Dragon Only). . . . . . . **x 25**

Example "This Year" hand

22 444 DDDD 666 88 . . . . **x 25**

Example 2468 hand

FFFFFF 333 + 888 = 11 or **FFFFFF** 333 **+ 888 = 11**. . . . . **x 30**

Example Change-Up hand

55555 4444 333 22 (These Nos. Only) . . . . **x 45**

Example Quints hand

111 222 **333 444 55** (Any 3 Suits, Any 5 Consecutive Nos.) . . . . **x 25**

Example Consecutive Run hand

11 33 **11 33 55 1111** (Any 3 Suits, Kong 1, 3, or 5) . . . . **c 30**

Example 13579 hand

FF NNN SSS 11 11 11 (Pairs Any Like Odd Nos.) . . . . **x 35**

Example Winds=Dragons hand

3333 66 **DD** 66 **9999** (Any 3 Suits). . . . . **x 30**

Example 369 hand

11 22 33 44 55 66 77 (Any Run 7 Pairs) . . . . **c 45**

Example Singles And Pairs hand

Various types of One Bams.

Various types of White Dragons.

Various types of Green Dragons.

Various types of Red Dragons.

Typical type of flower tiles.

Alternate types of flower tiles.

Additional type of flower tiles.

Various types of American jokers.

Chinese jokers ("100 uses").

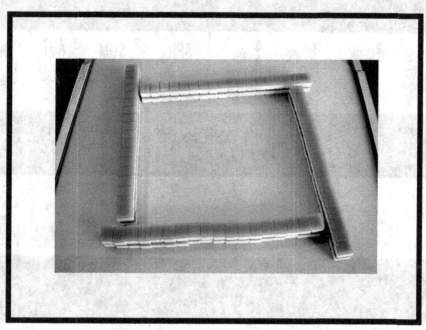

Chinese walls are eighteen stacks long.

American walls are nineteen stacks long.

34. Lesser Honors and Knitted Tiles
   a. Value: 12 points.
   b. Any 5 or 6 single honors (winds and dragons), and either 8 or 9 tiles from a knitted straight.
   c. May not combine with Concealed Hand or All Types. May combine with Knitted Straight. If self-picked, Fully Concealed may be added.

35. Knitted Straight
   a. Value: 12 points.
   b. A special straight made of knitted sets: 1-4-7 in one suit, 2-5-8 in another suit, and 3-6-9 in the third suit.
   c. May not combine with Edge Wait or Closed Wait. May combine with All Chows and with Lesser Honors and Knitted Tiles.

36. Upper Four
   a. Value: 12 points.
   b. Hand consisting solely of 6's, 7's, 8's, and 9's.

37. Lower Four
   a. Value: 12 points.
   b. Hand consisting solely of 1's, 2's, 3's, and 4's.

38. Big Three Winds
   a. Value: 12 points.
   b. Hand contains pungs or kongs of three winds.

39. Mixed Straight
   a. Value: 8 points.
   b. One through 9, made up of three sequential chows in three suits (1-2-3 in one suit, 4-5-6 in a second suit, and 7-8-9 in the third suit).

40. Reversible Tiles
   a. Value: 8 points.
   b. Hand composed solely of tiles that look the same whether right side up or upside down. If using a set with Western indices in the upper corner, the indices are ignored. The vertically symmetrical tiles are the 2, 4, 5, 6, 8, and 9 of Bams, the 1, 2, 3, 4, 5, 8, and 9 of Dots, and the White Dragon.

41. Mixed Triple Chow

a. Value: 8 points.

b. Three chows, all composed of the same numerical sequences, in three suits.

42. Mixed Shifted Pungs

a. Value: 8 points.

b. Three pungs of numerical values one higher than the other, in three suits.

43. Chicken Hand

a. Value: 8 points.

b. A three-suit hand with an honor pair waiting on a two-way call, won by discard. Disregarding flowers, if this hand was not listed here as being worth 8 points, it would otherwise earn 0 points. Must not include a terminal pung (that would make it worth 1 point). Must not be all pungs, all chows, or all pairs. Anything that earns even 1 point ruins the hand's status as Chicken Hand.

44. Last Tile Draw

a. Value: 8 points.

b. Going out by self-pick with the very last tile in the wall.

c. May not combine with Self-Drawn (implied).

45. Last Tile Claim

a. Value: 8 points.

b. Going out on a discard that had been the very last tile in the wall.

46. Out with Replacement Tile

a. Value: 8 points.

b. Winning on a tile taken as a kong replacement tile. (Not awarded for going out on a flower replacement tile, ever. If the kong replacement tile is a flower, and the flower replacement tile is the winning tile, Out with Replacement Tile is not awarded.)

c. May not combine with Self-Drawn (implied).

47. Robbing the Kong

a. Value: 8 points.

b. Winning on a tile used by another player to promote an exposed pung to a kong.

    c. Treated as win by discard.

    d. May not combine with Last Tile.

48. Two Concealed Kongs

    a. Value: 8 points.

    b. Two kongs, made the hard way. (Note: originally, Two Concealed Kongs was valued at 6 points, but this was changed in 2006 by the WMO.)

49. All Pungs

    a. Value: 6 points.

    b. Hand composed of four pungs or kongs and a pair.

50. Half Flush

    a. Value: 6 points.

    b. A hand containing some honors, and suit tiles of just one suit. In some books, this type of hand is referred to as "clean" or "semipure."

51. Mixed Shifted Chows

    a. Value: 6 points.

    b. Three chows in three suits, in which the first tile of each chow is "shifted" up one number from the previous chow. (A very important pattern, much used by expert players.)

52. All Types

    a. Value: 6 points.

    b. Hand contains sets (including pairs) of each suit, and winds and dragons.

    c. May combine with Seven Pairs.

53. Melded Hand

    a. Value: 6 points.

    b. A hand with four exposed sets (pungs, kongs, and/or chows), won by discard.

    c. May not combine with Single Wait (implied).

54. Two Dragons

    a. Value: 6 points.

    b. Two pungs or kongs of dragons.

55. Outside Hand

    a. Value: 4 points.

    b. A hand that includes terminals or honors in each set, including the pair.

56. Fully Concealed Hand
  a. Value: 4 points.
  b. A hand with no exposures prior to winning, won by self-pick.
  c. May not combine with Self-Drawn or Concealed Hand (both are implied).

57. Two Melded Kongs
  a. Value: 4 points.
  b. If the hand has two melded kongs, 4 points are awarded. If the hand has one melded kong and one concealed kong, 6 points are awarded (having added the 2 points for Concealed Kong).

58. Last Tile ("Case Tile")
  a. Value: 4 points.
  b. Winning on the "case tile" (the last or fourth tile of its particular kind) when all players can plainly see that it's so.

59. Dragon Pung
  a. Value: 2 points.
  b. A pung of any dragon.
  c. If it's a kong, the point(s) for Melded or Concealed Kong may be added.

60. Prevalent Wind
  a. Value: 2 points.
  b. A pung of the wind corresponding to the wind of the current round. The rounds are E, S, W, and N respectively. Some players may refer to this as the "Prevailing Wind" or the "Round Wind."

61. Seat Wind
  a. Value: 2 points.
  b. A pung of the wind corresponding to the seat of the winner. Counterclockwise starting with the dealer, the seat winds are E, S, W, N. Some players may refer to this as "Own Wind."

62. Concealed Hand
  a. Value: 2 points.
  b. Having no exposures and winning by discard.

63. All Chows
   a. Value: 2 points.
   b. A hand with four chows, in which the pair contains neither winds nor dragons. The Chinese call this hand *"Pin Hu."*
   c. May not combine with No Honors (implied).

64. Tile Hog
   a. Value: 2 points.
   b. Using all 4 of a particular tile, without using them in a kong of any kind. (The tiles might be used in a pung and a chow, or as two pairs.)

65. Double Pung
   a. Value: 2 points.
   b. Two pungs of suit tiles, of the same number in two suits.

66. Two Concealed Pungs
   a. Value: 2 points.
   b. Hand contains two pungs, made the hard way (without melding).

67. Concealed Kong
   a. Value: 2 points.
   b. A kong made the hard way, melded facedown.

68. All Simples
   a. Value: 2 points.
   b. A hand with no honors or terminals. (The simples are the numbered suit tiles from 2 through 8.)

69. Pure Double Chow
   a. Value: 1 point.
   b. Two identical chows (same numerical sequence, same suit). Some players call this "Twin Sisters" or "Twins."

70. Mixed Double Chow.
   a. Value: 1 point.
   b. Two similar chows (same numerical sequence, but different suits). Some players call this "Sisters."

71. Short Straight
   a. Value: 1 point.
   b. Two sequential chows, forming 6 sequential numbers in one suit.

72. Two Terminal Chows
a. Value: 1 point.
b. Opposite-end terminal chows (1-2-3 and 7-8-9) in one suit.

73. Pung of Terminals or Honors
a. Value: 1 point.
b. A pung or kong of any wind or any terminal. (The terminals are the 1's and 9's of a suit.)
c. May combine with Prevalent Wind or Seat Wind.

74. Melded Kong
a. Value: 1 point.
b. An exposed kong (whether made by discard or by promoting an exposed pung).

75. One Voided Suit
a. Value: 1 point.
b. A hand that has tiles from two suits, lacking any tiles of the third suit. Winds or dragons may also be present in the hand.

76. No Honors
a. Value: 1 point.
b. A hand composed entirely of suit tiles.

77. Edge Wait
a. Value: 1 point.
b. Waiting with an incomplete terminal chow in which the terminal tile and its nearest neighbor are both present, waiting for the missing tile to complete the chow and go mahjong. For example, holding 1 and 2 and waiting for the 3, or holding 9 and 8 and waiting for the 7.

78. Closed Wait
a. Value: 1 point.
b. Card players may think of this as waiting on an "inside straight." Holding two tiles separated by a 1-tile gap, waiting for the missing tile to fill the gap, complete the chow, and go mahjong. For example, holding 5 and 7, waiting for the 6.

79. Single Wait

a. Value: 1 point.

b. Waiting while holding a single tile, waiting for its mate to complete the pair in a typical four-sets-and-a-pair hand.

80. Self-Drawn

a. Value: 1 point.

b. Winning by picking the winning tile from the wall. Also called "self-pick."

81. Flower Tiles

a. Value: 1 point.

b. After winning, each flower or season tile among the winner's melds is worth 1 point.

c. Flowers do not count toward the 8-point minimum score requirement (the hand must be worth 8 points on its own merits, without regard to how many flowers the player has).

d. It is permitted to discard flowers rather than meld them (player must still say *"Hua"* or *"Hwar"*).

e. Winning upon taking a flower replacement earns a point for Self-Drawn (it does not qualify as winning upon taking a kong replacement).

B. How to Play Chinese Official Mahjong

DETERMINE SEATS

If you're playing in the home, you'll use a standard card table or mahjong table, with four chairs in a well-lit area. If players have drinks or snacks, small side tables at the corners of the game table are a good idea.

At a tournament, when it's time to go to your table, look on your handout for your seat assignment. It's probably a chart, listing table numbers and player numbers. Find your table and sit in any seat. A referee

checks to ensure that the correct players are seated at the table. When all players are present, seating is decided by using 4 wind tiles. Usually, when you come to the table, all tiles are neatly arranged, and all except 4 wind tiles are facedown.

To begin, someone (anyone) takes the 4 wind tiles and turns them facedown and shuffles them. The official rules do not specify the procedure that must be used, but typically, someone is chosen to roll the dice (the one foreigner, when three Chinese players are present, or the one woman, when three men are present, or the oldest person, or the guest when playing in someone's home, for example). The roll of the dice indicates which player will take the first facedown tile (counting counterclockwise from the roller, starting with the roller as "one"). The indicated player picks any facedown tile, then each other player, taking turns counterclockwise around the table, picks a facedown tile. Each player turns his tile faceup to see what seat the player is to sit in. Look around the tournament hall; one wall is marked with the Chinese character for East (東). The player with the East tile sits with his or her back toward the east wall (in the seat closest to the east wall). The player with the South tile sits to East's right; the player with the West tile sits opposite East; the player with the North tile sits to East's left.

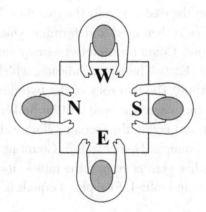

At a tournament, East is designated scorekeeper. He or she writes the names of the players on the scoresheet, according to the determined seating positions.

BUILD WALLS
The 4 wind tiles are put back among the other tiles facedown, and the 144 tiles (the standard Chinese set, without any joker tiles) are shuffled thoroughly. Each player pulls tiles toward him and builds them into a wall eighteen stacks long and two tiles high.

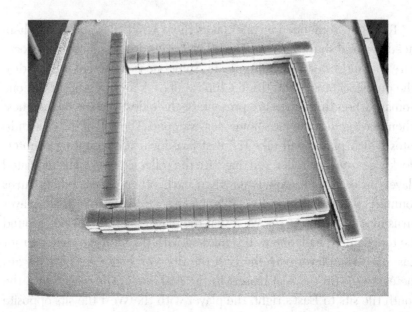

DEAL

The player sitting in the east seat rolls the two dice. The number indicated by the two dice is then used to determine which player shall roll the dice a second time. Count counterclockwise around the table, starting with the dealer (East). The count indicates which player shall roll the dice a second time. The two rolls of the two dice are then added together to determine where the wall will be broken, counting clockwise from the rightmost end of the second roller's wall.

Let's look at an example. Dealer rolls 5. Counting from "one" (himself), dealer counts five players around the table—it's his own seat. He takes the dice again, and rolls 4. Five plus 4 equals 9.

Dealer rolls first.   *Indicated player rolls.*   *Add the two rolls,*
break wall.

Dealer, counting nine to the left (beginning with the right end of his own wall, he being the second roller), arrives at the ninth stack on the east wall. Dealer makes a break to the left of the ninth stack, so that there are nine stacks to the right of the break.

Now the dealer takes the next two stacks (4 tiles), continuing to remove tiles clockwise from the break. South (the player at East's right, in other words the player counterclockwise from the dealer) takes the next two stacks; then West takes two stacks; then North takes two stacks.

Dealer takes two stacks.   South takes two stacks.   West takes two stacks.

Now each player is holding 4 tiles. Dealer takes the last 4 tiles (two stacks). The dealer's wall has now been depleted, so the next wall to be used is North's wall (at the dealer's left). South takes two stacks; West takes two stacks; North takes two stacks. Now each player is holding 8 tiles. The procedure is repeated until each player is holding 12 tiles.

North takes two stacks.   East takes—second time.   South takes two stacks.

West takes two stacks.   North takes two stacks.   East takes—third time.

South takes two stacks.   *West takes two stacks.*   *North takes two stacks.*

East then takes the top tiles from the first and third stacks ("one and three"). South takes the tile at the end of the wall; West takes the upper tile from the stack at the end of the wall; North takes the tile at the end of the wall.

Now East is holding 14 tiles and each other player is holding 13 tiles.

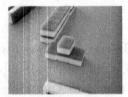

East takes "1 and 3."   *South takes end tile.*   *West takes top end tile.*

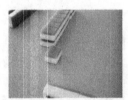

North takes end tile.   *Players arrange their tiles.*   *East discards a tile.*

Throughout this procedure, actions occur in two directions simultaneously: **counterclockwise** (the players taking tiles in turn) and **clockwise** (the tiles disappearing from the wall). During the course of play, players always take turns counterclockwise (even during the deal)—and tiles are always removed clockwise from the wall (even during the deal).

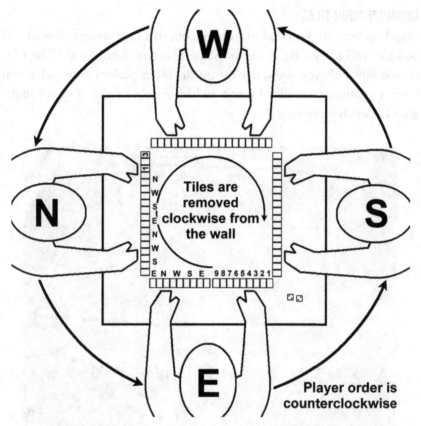

Players take counterclockwise turns removing tiles clockwise from the wall.

FLOWERS

When you see flower tiles in your dealt tiles, expose them immediately. Flowers are not used in the hand (they add 1 point each, for a player who wins). After the deal, the dealer will draw flower replacements from the back end of the wall (the opposite end used during the deal), check them for more flowers, then when holding no more flowers, gesture to the player to his right. Each player in turn replaces flowers, checking the replacement tiles for more flowers.

When replacing a flower tile, it's required that you speak. When playing with American players, you could say "Flower," but when playing internationally, it's best to use the Chinese word, *"Hua"* (pronounced *"Hwar"*).

ORGANIZE YOUR TILES

Stand up your tiles on end in front of you, in a neat straight line. (Or if you use racks, lean them on the sloped surface facing you.) The tiles should face only you—you don't want the other players to see what you have. Organize your tiles by suit and by number value. Do not make gaps between groupings.

Now you're ready to play mahjong.

THE GOAL

The goal of the game is to go out with a complete mahjong hand, valued at 8 or more points without regard to flowers, before anybody else does. It's a lot like the card games of the rummy family. A complete 14-tile mahjong hand is usually composed of four sets and a pair.

What's a "Set"?

Excluding pairs for a moment, there are three kinds of sets: pungs and chows, both composed of 3 tiles, and kongs, composed of 4 tiles.

A pung is 3 identical tiles. For example, three Two Dot tiles is called a "pung" of Two Dots. Unlike playing cards and rummy, you cannot make a group with a 2 in one suit, a 2 in another suit, and a 2 in a third suit. (Such a set is called a Knitted Pung, and it's used only in Western-style mahjong, a variant not described in this book.)

Two example pungs: a pung of Green Dragons and a pung of Four Dots.

A chow is three numbered tiles in numerical sequence. For example, if you have a Six Bam and a Seven Bam and an Eight Bam. You cannot make a chow with tiles in different suits; they must all be in the same suit (the exception is the "Knitted Chow," to be discussed later). And you cannot make a chow with dragons or winds (the tiles in a chow *must* all be numbered suit tiles).

Two example chows: a 123 of Craks, and a 678 of Bams.

A kong is 4 identical tiles (all 4 tiles with a particular value and suit, for instance).

Here is an example hand made of four sets and a pair:

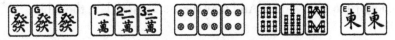

An example hand composed of: a pung (dragons), a chow (Craks),
a pung (Dots), a chow (Bams), and a pair (winds).

A hand does not have to be two chows, two pungs, and a pair (as in the example above). It can be four pungs and a pair, or four chows and a pair, or three chows and a pung and a pair, or two pungs, a kong, a chow, and a pair. . . . Any four sets and a pair.

There are also other types of hands permitted in the Chinese Official game: Seven Pairs, Knitted Chows, and unique honors and terminals.

These other types of hands are described later. If you are a beginner, you should start by striving to make regular four-sets-and-a-pair hands, and add the other hand types to your repertoire as your familiarity with the game grows.

HOW TO PLAY

After the deal, the dealer is holding 14 tiles, and everybody else is holding 13 tiles. So, to begin, it's the dealer's turn. The dealer examines the tiles in his hand to see if his hand is already a winner or not. Is the hand composed of four groups and a pair, with enough *fan* to score 8 points? If so, dealer wins instantly. (That is a rare occurrence.) If dealer's hand is not yet composed of four groups and a pair worth 8 points, then the dealer must discard a tile.

DISCARDING

The dealer must take any 1 tile from the hand and place it faceup on the table in front of him (between his wall and the center of the table).

Choosing a tile to discard is where the strategy lies. Each player strives to make a complete mahjong hand, utilizing enough of the official scoring elements to add up to a minimum of 8 points. The player discards a tile that cannot be used to achieve this goal.

In the Chinese Official game, discards must be placed in rows of six before each player to facilitate other players reading the history of the game. Discards are arranged left to right, the rows arranged center outward.

Having discarded, the dealer now has 13 tiles in his hand. The dealer's turn is now over. And now there's a discard on the table.

Can I Take Someone Else's Discard?

The normal flow of play is that the players, in turn, pick and discard. But it sometimes happens that a player's discarded tile helps further someone's hand toward completion. When it happens that a discard helps further your hand toward completion, you may take it, provided (1) that it is the most recent discard, (2) that no more than 3 seconds have passed, and if you need the tile to complete a chow, (3) that the player at your left is the one who discarded it.

You can take only the tile discarded by the most recent player. If there are 5 or 6 tiles lying in the center of the table, only the newest one is up for grabs. And it is available (the "window of opportunity" is open) for only 3 seconds until the next player makes a move. You have to be quick in mahjong!

Unlike some rummy rules, you cannot take a discard and place it in your hand. You are only allowed to take someone's discard if it completes a set or if it completes the hand. Discards may be taken only to complete a chow or a pung or kong, or to complete the hand for mahjong. There is a price for taking a discard to complete a set—the completed set must be exposed for all to see, giving them clues as to what you are doing.

Taking a Discard to Make a Chow

Chows may be declared only on the player's own turn, using a tile discarded by the previous player (the player to the left). When taking a discard to make a chow, the action must be verbalized first. In America or Europe, it's okay to say "Chow," but if playing in Asia it may be better to say "*Chur*" (Chinese) or "*Chi*" (Japanese).

When a player wishes to chow, he should pause a beat, in case another player might want to pung the tile. It's not just courtesy to pause. It's also good strategy. If another player were to claim the tile for pung, that player would get the tile, and if both of you had spoken, others would know what you wanted.

Then, after speaking, expose the 2 tiles from your hand, take the discard and put it with the others to form the exposure. The taken tile is rotated 90 degrees and placed at the left side of the exposure, so that everyone can see which tile was claimed, and from whom.

The rotated tile is always the tile that was taken. The tile being at the left indicates that it was taken from the player to the left. The rotated tile in a chow is always at the left, regardless of its numerical value, because a chow can only be made from the player to the left.

Taking a Discard to Make a Pung

To take a discard to make a pung (three of a kind), you may take the discard instantly when it appears on the table, regardless of whose turn it is. If you have a pair of East Winds, and somebody discards a third East Wind, you are allowed to claim it even if it's not your turn. Say "Pung," expose the 2 tiles from your hand, and take the discard. The taken tile is rotated 90 degrees and placed within the pung so as to indicate which of the three opponents it came from. If the player at your left discarded the tile, the rotated tile is placed at the left of the pung. If the discard came from your opposite opponent, the rotated tile is placed in the middle of the pung. If the discard came from the player at your right, the rotated tile is placed at the right of the pung.

Taking a Discard to Make a Kong

A discard can be taken to make a kong only if you have a concealed pung in the hand. If you have an exposed pung on the table, you may not take a discard to promote the pung to a kong.

If you have a concealed pung and someone discards the fourth tile, you are permitted to call it for exposure. (It's not always a good idea to do this, for strategic reasons discussed later.) Use the same procedure as for making a pung (above), but note that kongs pose a unique problem requiring an extra step. The unique problem is that the overall tile count of the hand, 14 tiles, usually in four sets and a pair, becomes problematic when one of the sets is 4 tiles rather than 3.

It won't be possible to make a hand of "four sets and a pair" (as previously defined) using just 14 tiles, when one of the sets uses 4 tiles. To solve the problem, the full hand will now have to contain 15 tiles rather than 14. So when making a kong, the player must perform an extra step before discarding. The player must meld the kong (announcing "Kong"), then take an extra tile (called a kong replacement tile), from the back end of the wall (the opposite end to the usual end from which tiles are picked), and place it in the hand, before discarding to end the turn.

Taking a Discard for Mahjong

To take a discard to win, you must first speak. If playing with American players, it *may* be permissible to say "Mahjong," but the official practice is to say the Chinese word, *"Hu."* You may win on any player's discard (except your own), regardless of whose turn it is, and regardless of whether the tile completes a chow, pung, kong, or pair—or, for special hands not using the usual four-sets-and-a-pair structure, to fill the hand as a single tile.

After Taking a Discard

After exposing the completed grouping, if your hand is not yet a complete and valid mahjong hand, you have to discard a tile. Be quick about it so the game can move on. If you took a discard to make a pung, the player to your right goes next. (The order of play is disrupted when someone makes a pung or a kong.)

Instead of Taking a Discard

You don't always want to take a discard. Because there are 4 of each tile, there could well be other chances to complete the hand, without having to show other players what you are doing. You might pick a better tile than the one someone else discarded.

When the tile you picked gives you a complete chow or pung in the hand, it is not necessary (or permissible) to expose the set. Keep your concealed sets a happy secret from your opponents. Only sets made by taking a discard need to be exposed.

The normal flow of play is that the players all take turns, picking from the wall and discarding. This order of play may be thought of as flowing downhill; the player at one's right is called the "lower" seat; the player at one's left is called the "upper" seat.

Usually, when a player has discarded a tile, you cannot or do not want to claim it. After the player at your left has discarded, you must then reach for the next tile on the end of the wall and take it. If the tile does not give you a complete and valid mahjong hand (as it usually does not), you must discard a tile to complete your turn. Try to think ahead about what tile you will discard on your next turn so the game will progress quickly. Try to finish your turn within 10 seconds, and no more. The game is more fun if it moves smoothly and quickly.

FLOWERS

If you pick a flower, you may immediately expose it and draw a replacement tile from the back end of the wall. You must verbalize the action as described previously. It is permissible to keep a flower in the hand and use it as a safe discard later in the dangerous last few turns of a game.

KONGS

There are two ways you can self-pick a kong: concealed and exposed.

It sometimes happens that you have an exposed pung, and you then pick the fourth tile. When this happens, say "Kong," add the tile to the pung (promoting it to a kong), and take the replacement tile from the back end of the wall. This is an exposed kong. Everyone can see that you have a kong, and what tiles are in it.

You might have a concealed pung in the hand, and then pick the fourth tile. When you are making a typical four-sets-and-a-pair hand, it's necessary to declare the kong so you can get the replacement tile, repairing the hand's integrity as previously described. But it would be unfair to have to show others what's in your kong, so you are permitted to meld the 4 tiles facedown in the area where you normally place exposures and flowers. This is called a concealed kong, and it's more valuable than an exposed kong. Everybody can see that you have a kong, but nobody except you knows what tiles are in it. Having a melded concealed kong does not disqualify the whole hand from being regarded as concealed.

You may only make a concealed kong on a turn that began with your picking a tile from the wall. It's not permitted to kong on a turn that began by taking a discard to chow or pung; the kong move would have to wait until the next turn.

PROGRESSION OF PLAY

Play progresses counterclockwise around the table in mahjong. On your turn, you start with 13 tiles. Then you take a fourteenth tile into your hand (usually by picking it from the wall; sometimes you take a discard and expose a grouping). If your hand is not yet complete (it usually isn't), you discard a tile. Now you have 13 tiles again. That's the way a typical turn works. Then it's the next player's turn.

This sequence of events is repeated (someone may call a tile for exposure now and then) until either someone wins or the tiles in the wall have all been taken.

SOMEBODY WINS

The moment someone has a complete valid hand, he or she must declare it aloud. If you're not going to be playing in an official tournament, and if the others in your group don't mind, you can simply say "Mahjong." But in an official tournament, it's the custom to declare it in Chinese: *"Hu."*

Then the hand is displayed for all to see, with the winning tile set apart so all can see. It's not permitted to put the winning tile among the other hand tiles prior to exposure (that's a punishable offense). The winner must explain how his hand is scored. The other players verify that it is correct. If playing for chips, nonwinners pay the winner. If playing on paper, the scorekeeper notes the win and subtracts points from nonwinners, then shows the scorecard to others for their verification.

OR NOBODY WINS

The moment there are no more tiles left in the wall, nobody can continue playing. It's a wall game. Everybody throws in their tiles, shuffles them, and builds walls for the next hand.

GAME STRUCTURE

After a hand has been played (whether someone wins or not, and regardless of who wins, dealer or nondealer), the dice always pass to the player to the right of the previous dealer.

After the deal has passed around the table completely (each of the players has dealt), one round has been completed. A complete game consists of four rounds. The rounds are named for the four major compass directions, in this order: East, South, West, North (the same order as the seats around the table).

Upon completion of the fourth hand of the fourth (North) round, or when the tournament judges ring a bell, the game ends. Scores are tallied to determine the winner of the game.

SEAT ROTATION

In an official tournament, the players rotate seats upon completion of each round. This mixes up the "feeding order." The player at your left "feeds" you tiles that you can use for a chow, and you "feed" chowable tiles to the player at your right. In a game that can last 2 hours or more, it's desirable to mix up the order so that a player is not always stuck with the same players at his left and his right.

After the first round, East and South switch seats, while North and West switch seats. After the second round, East moves to West, South moves to North, West moves to South, North moves to East. After the third round, East and South switch seats, and North and West switch seats.

The following table shows the seat rotation order for each player during the four rounds of a game.

East Player rotation	E-S-N-W (right, across, left)
South Player rotation	S-E-W-N (left, across, right)
West Player rotation	W-N-E-S (clockwise around the table)
North Player rotation	N-W-S-E (counterclockwise around the table)

This way, each player sits in each position around the table, and each player "feeds" each other player, and is in turn "fed" by each other player, during a game session.

CONFLICTING CLAIMS

It sometimes happens that two players claim 1 discarded tile. When one player wants a discard to make a chow, and one wants it to make a pung, then the punger gets the tile (claims for a pung trump claims for a chow).

When one player wants a discard to make an exposure, and another player wants it for a win, then the winner gets the tile (claims for a win trump claims for an exposed set).

When two players both want a discard to win, then the player whose turn would come sooner in the order of play gets the win. Let's say player one throws a tile, and player three and player four both want it. Player three's turn would normally come before player four's turn, so player three gets the tile.

BEGINNERS' MOST COMMONLY MISUNDERSTOOD RULES

- Going counterclockwise around the table, players' seat winds are East, South, West, North. It does not correspond to the expected compass directions on a map (East, North, West, South).

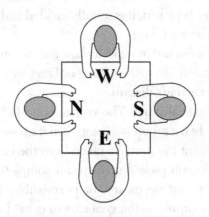

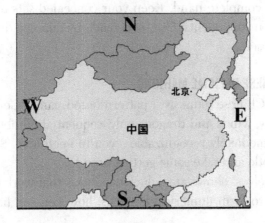

- In mahjong, there is no such thing as a chow of 4 or more tiles in numerical sequence. A chow is three sequential suit tiles only.
- There is no such thing as a chow made from "one of each dragon." Chows may use suit tiles only.
- There is no such thing as a kong made from "one of each wind." A kong is 4 identical tiles only. And there is no such thing as a chow made from three different winds; chows may use suit tiles only.
- There is no such thing as a pair, pung, kong, or chow of flowers. Flowers are exposed singly and are not counted toward the tile count in the hand. The numbers that may exist on some flower tiles are meaningless. The numbers on flower tiles are meaningful only in certain other variants of mahjong (notably, Chinese Classical). When a flower is picked, it is usually melded and replaced from the back end of the wall.
- You can take a discard to make a chow only when it is thrown by the player at your left. To make a pung or kong, or to declare mahjong, you can take anyone's discard.
- A kong is a special pung. The typical hand is "four groups and a pair"—and when a group is a kong, then it messes up the tile count. So a replacement tile must be taken from the back end of the wall.
- When the tile you picked gives you a complete chow or pung in the hand, it is not necessary (or permissible) to expose the set. Mahjong isn't rummy—the goal isn't to get rid of your tiles, it's to build a complete hand. Keep your concealed sets a happy secret from your opponents. Only sets made by taking a discard need to be exposed.

SCORING CHINESE OFFICIAL MAHJONG

The official Chinese game is a pattern-based game. Certain patterns (one suit only, winds and dragons only, sequential numbers, reversible tiles) are immediately recognizable, even to beginners. Some patterns are more subtle and take some getting used to.

By themselves, chows are valueless. Chows that work together with other chows to form numerical patterns, however, can have value collectively. Pungs of terminals, winds, and dragons are more valuable than pungs of simples (tiles numbered from 2 to 8). Kongs have value, whether concealed or exposed.

Score is also earned by certain ways of going out. Winning by picking the winning tile is always more valuable. Winning by discard is valuable only when the rest of the player's hand had also all been made by discards. Winning on the fourth tile of its kind, or the last tile in the wall, are other ways of winning that earn the player extra points. The hand earns points if it had been concealed prior to declaring mahjong.

Each of these ways of earning points (patterns, valuable sets, and ways of going out) may be referred to as "scoring elements" collectively. There is a list of 81 scoring elements in the official Chinese game. The Chinese call these scoring elements *"fan."*

Only the player who makes mahjong scores points. When the player declares mahjong, the player may add up each of the scoring elements present in the hand to arrive at the hand's score. There are certain rules that must be obeyed in adding up the scoring elements, described below.

Scoring Basics

1. The winning hand must score a minimum of 8 points, *not including points for flowers;*
2. Adding a point for each flower to the hand's score, the score total is called the "basic points;"
3. When the hand is obtained by discard,
   a. Discarder pays basic points plus 8 "extra points";
   b. Non-discarders only pay 8 extra points each;
4. When the hand is obtained by self-pick, *all* nonwinners pay the winner the basic points plus the 8 points.
5. Penalty points, if any, are subtracted prior to payment.

Payment

Points are paid on paper or by using chips. If using chips, each player starts with 500 points. A suggested 500-point breakdown for chips is as follows:

100-point chips	2	200
50-point chips	3	150
10-point chips	12	120
1-point chips	30	30
		500

THE SCORING ELEMENTS ("*FAN*")

Score may be earned by characteristics of the winning hand: special patterns, the method of going out, concealment, etc. There are 81 different scoring elements (called *fan* in Chinese), and they earn points based on their difficulty or rarity. Scoring elements may be combined unless prohibited by the scoring principles or unless specifically contra-indicated in the description in the list. The *fan* are listed (and numbered) in the order used in the original Chinese rule book; other numbering orders may be seen in other books.

1.   Big Four Winds   88 points
Pungs or kongs of all four of the winds. May not combine with Big Three Winds, Little Four Winds, All Pungs, Seat Wind, Prevalent Wind, or Pung of Terminals or Honors.

2.   Big Three Dragons   88 points
Pungs or kongs of all three of the dragons. May not combine with Dragon Pungs or Two Dragons.

3.   All Green   88 points
Tiles are all green. The only tiles that can be used in this hand (in any combination) are the 2, 3, 4, 6, or 8 of Bams and the Green Dragon. May be combined with Half Flush or Full Flush. When combined with Seven Pairs, Tile Hog may not be added.

4. Nine Gates   88 points

Tiles of one suit only, with concealed pungs of both terminals (1's and 9's) and one of each simple, and (as the final winning tile) a duplicate of any tile in the hand. Prior to obtaining the final tile, the hand was concealed, waiting for any tile in the suit to win (a nine-way wait). May not be combined with Full Flush (implied), Concealed, Edge Wait, Closed Wait, Single Wait, or Pung of Terminals or Honors. If self-picked, Fully Concealed may be added.

5. Four Kongs   88 points

A hand made with four kongs, regardless how many are concealed or exposed (points for concealment may be added; 2 points for One Concealed Kong, 8 points for Two Concealed Kongs, 16 points for Three Concealed Pungs, 64 points for Four Concealed Pungs). May not be combined with Single Wait (implied).

6. Seven Shifted Pairs   88 points

Tiles of one suit only, forming seven sequentially numbered pairs. May not combine with Full Flush, Concealed Hand, or Single Wait. If self-picked, Fully Concealed may be added.

7. Thirteen Orphans   88 points

One of each terminal and honor, plus a duplicate of any. Points for All Types, Concealed Hand, or Single Wait may not be added. If self-picked, Fully Concealed may be added.

8.   All Terminals   64 points

Hand consists solely of 1's and 9's. May not be combined with All Pungs, Outside Hand, or No Honors. Double Pung and Triple Pung may be combined. When combined with Seven Pairs, Tile Hog may not be added.

9.   Little Four Winds   64 points

Pungs of three winds, and a pair of the fourth. May combine with Seat Wind and Prevalent Wind, but not with Big Three Winds or Pung of Terminals or Honors.

10.   Little Three Dragons   64 points

Pungs of two dragons, and a pair of the third. May not combine with Dragon Pung or Two Dragons.

11.   All Honors   64 points

Pairs, pungs, or kongs of winds and dragons only. May not combine with All Pungs, Outside Hand, or Pung of Terminals or Honors. Points for Dragon Pung, Prevalent Wind, Seat Wind may be added.

12.   Four Concealed Pungs   64 points

Four pungs, all made the hard way (without melding). May not combine with Concealed Hand or All Pungs. If self-picked, Fully Concealed may be added.

13.   Pure Terminal Chows   64 points

Two 1-2-3 chows and two 7-8-9 chows, and a pair of 5's, all in the same suit. May not combine with Full Flush, All Chows, Seven Pairs, Pure Double Chow, Mixed Double Chow, or Two Terminal Chows.

14.   Quadruple Chow   48 points

Four identical chows (same numerical sequence, same suit). May not combine with Tile Hog, Pure Triple Chow, Pure Double Chow, or Pure Shifted Pungs.

15.   Four Pure Shifted Pungs   48 points

Four pungs in one suit, each shifted up one number from the last. May not combine with All Pungs or Pure Triple Chow.

16.   Four Shifted Chows   32 points

Four chows in one suit, all shifted up one number from the last, or all shifted up two numbers from the last. May not combine with Short Straight or Two Terminal Chows.

17.   Three Kongs   32 points

A hand with three kongs. Points for concealment may be added (2 points for One Concealed Kong, 8 points for Two Concealed Kongs, or 16 points for Three Concealed Pungs, if all kongs are concealed).

18.   All Terminals and Honors   32 points

Pairs, pungs, or kongs of terminals, winds, and dragons only. May not combine with All Pungs, Outside Hand, or Pung of Terminals or Honors.

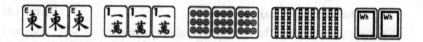

19.   Seven Pairs   24 points

Seven pairs of any tile. May not combine with Concealed Hand or Single Wait. May combine with All Types and Tile Hog. If self-picked, Fully Concealed may be added.

20.   Greater Honors and Knitted Tiles   24 points

One of each dragon and wind, plus any 7 tiles of an incomplete Knitted Straight. (A Knitted Straight is 1-4-7 in one suit, 2-5-8 in another suit, and 3-6-9 in the third suit.) May not combine with Concealed Hand or All Types (both are implied).

21.   All Even Pungs   **24 points**

A hand formed with four pungs and a pair of even-numbered suit tiles. May not combine with All Pungs or All Simples.

22.   Full Flush ("Pure")   **24 points**

A hand using tiles of one suit only. May not combine with No Honors.

23.   Pure Triple Chow   **24 points**

Three identical chows. May not combine with Pure Shifted Pungs or Pure Double Chow.

24.   Pure Shifted Pungs   **24 points**

Three sequentially numbered pungs in one suit. May not combine with Pure Triple Chow.

25.   Upper Tiles   **24 points**

A hand composed entirely of 7's, 8's, and 9's. May not combine with No Honors.

26.   Middle Tiles   **24 points**

A hand composed entirely of 4's, 5's, and 6's. May not combine with No Honors or All Simples.

27.   Lower Tiles   24 points

A hand composed entirely of 1's, 2's, and 3's. May not combine with No Honors.

28.   Pure Straight   16 points

One through 9 in one suit (three chows, end to end).

29.   Three-Suited Terminal Chows   16 points

Opposite-end terminal chows (1-2-3 and 7-8-9) in one suit, opposite-end terminal chows in a second suit, and a pair of 5's in the third suit. May not combine with All Chows, Two Terminal Chows, or Mixed Double Chow.

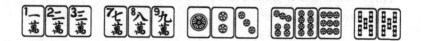

30.   Pure Shifted Chows   16 points

Three chows in one suit, each shifted up one number from the last, or each shifted up two numbers from the last.

31.   All Fives   16 points

Each set (including the pair) includes a 5. May not combine with All Simples.

32.   Triple Pung   **16 points**
Three pungs of the same number in each suit.

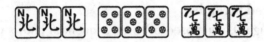

33.   Three Concealed Pungs   **16 points**
Three pungs made the hard way (without melding).

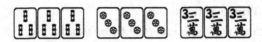

34.   Lesser Honors and Knitted Tiles   **12 points**
Any five or six single honors (winds and dragons), and either 8 or 9 tiles from a Knitted Straight. May combine with Knitted Straight. May not combine with Concealed Hand or All Types. If self-picked, Fully Concealed may be added.

35.   Knitted Straight   **12 points**
A special straight made of knitted sets: 1-4-7 in one suit, 2-5-8 in another suit, and 3-6-9 in the third suit. May combine with All Chows and with Lesser Honors and Knitted Tiles. May not combine with Edge Wait or Closed Wait.

36.   Upper Four   **12 points**
Hand consisting solely of 6's, 7's, 8's, and 9's.

37.   Lower Four   **12 points**
Hand consisting solely of 1's, 2's, 3's, and 4's.

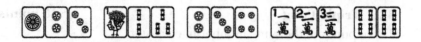

38.   Big Three Winds   12 points

Hand contains pungs or kongs of three winds.

39.   Mixed Straight   8 points

One through 9, composed of three sequential chows in three suits
(1-2-3 in one suit, 4-5-6 in a second suit, and 7-8-9 in the third
suit).

40.   Reversible Tiles   8 points

Hand composed solely of tiles that look the same whether right side
up or upside down. If using a set with Western indices in the upper
corner, the indices must be ignored. The vertically symmetrical tiles
are the 2, 4, 5, 6, 8, and 9 of Bams, the 1, 2, 3, 4, 5, 8, and 9 of Dots,
and the White Dragon.

41.   Mixed Triple Chow   8 points

Three chows, all composed of the same numerical sequences, in
three suits.

42.   Mixed Shifted Pungs   8 points

Three pungs of numerical values one higher than the other, in three
suits.

43.   Chicken Hand ("KFC")   8 points
A three-suit hand with an honor pair waiting on a two-way call, won by discard. Disregarding flowers, if this hand was not listed here as being worth 8 points, it would otherwise earn 0 points. Must not include a terminal pung (that would make it worth 1 point). Must not be all pungs, all chows, or all pairs. Anything that earns even 1 point ruins the hand's status as Chicken Hand.

44.   Last Tile Draw   8 points
Going out by self-pick with the very last tile in the wall. May not combine with Self-Drawn (implied).

45.   Last Tile Claim   8 points
Going out on a discard that had been the very last tile in the wall.

46.   Out with Replacement Tile   8 points
Winning on a tile taken as a kong replacement tile only. (Never awarded for going out on a flower replacement tile. If the kong replacement tile is a flower, and the flower replacement tile is the winning tile, Out with Replacement Tile is not awarded.) May not combine with Self-Drawn (implied).

47.   Robbing the Kong   8 points
Winning on a tile used by another player to promote an exposed pung to a kong. Treated as win by discard. May not combine with Last Tile.

48.   Two Concealed Kongs   8 points
Two kongs, made the hard way. (Note: originally, Two Concealed Kongs was valued at 6 points, but this was changed in 2006 by the WMO.)

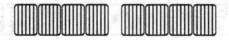

49. All Pungs   6 points
Hand composed of four pungs or kongs and a pair.

50. Half Flush   6 points
A hand containing some honors, and suit tiles of just one suit. In some books, this type of hand is referred to as "clean" or "semipure."

51. Mixed Shifted Chows   6 points
Three chows in three suits, in which the first tile of each chow is "shifted" up one number from the previous chow. A very important pattern, much used by expert players.

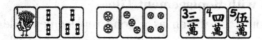

52. All Types   6 points
Hand contains sets (including pairs) of each suit, and winds and dragons. May combine with Seven Pairs.

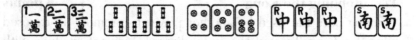

53. Melded Hand   6 points
A hand with four exposed sets (pungs, kongs, and/or chows), won by discard. May not combine with Single Wait (implied).

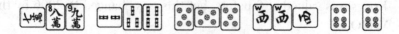

54.   Two Dragons   6 points
Two pungs or kongs of dragons.

55.   Outside Hand   4 points
A hand that includes terminals or honors in each set, including the pair.

56.   Fully Concealed Hand   4 points
A hand with no exposures prior to winning, won by self-pick. May not combine with Self-Drawn (implied).

57.   Two Melded Kongs   4 points
If the hand has two melded kongs, 4 points are awarded. If the hand has one melded kong and one concealed kong, 6 points are awarded (having added the 2 points for Concealed Kong).

58.   Last Tile ("Case Tile")   4 points
Winning on the "case tile" (the last or fourth tile of its particular kind) when all players can plainly see that it's so.

59.   Dragon Pung   2 points
A pung of any dragon. If it's a kong, the point for Melded Kong may be added.

60.   Prevalent Wind   **2 points**

A pung of the wind corresponding to the wind of the current round. Some players may refer to this as the "Prevailing Wind" or the "Round Wind." The rounds are E, S, W, and N respectively.

61.   Seat Wind   **2 points**

A pung of the wind corresponding to the seat of the winner. Counterclockwise starting with the dealer, the seat winds are E, S, W, N.

62.   Concealed Hand   **2 points**

Having no exposures and winning by discard.

63.   All Chows   **2 points**

A hand with four chows, in which the pair contains neither winds nor dragons. The Chinese call this hand *"Pin Hu."* May not combine with No Honors (implied).

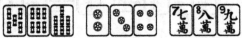

64.   Tile Hog   **2 points**

Using all four of a particular tile, without using them in a kong of any kind. (The tiles might be used in a pung and a chow, or as two pairs.)

65.   Double Pung   **2 points**

Two pungs of suit tiles, of the same number in two suits.

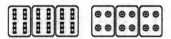

66.   Two Concealed Pungs   2 points
Hand contains two pungs, made the hard way (without melding).

67.   Concealed Kong   2 points
A kong made the hard way, melded facedown.

68.   All Simples   2 points
A hand with no honors or terminals. (The simples are the numbered
suit tiles from 2 through 8.)

69.   Pure Double Chow   1 point
Two identical chows (same numerical sequence, same suit). Some
players call this "Twin Sisters" or "Twins."

70.   Mixed Double Chow   1 point
Two similar chows (same numerical sequence, but different suits).
Some players call this "Sisters."

71.   Short Straight   1 point
Two sequential chows, forming six sequential numbers in one
suit.

72.   Two Terminal Chows   1 point

Opposite-end terminal chows (1-2-3 and 7-8-9) in one suit.

73.   Pung of Terminals or Honors   1 point

A pung of any wind or a pung of any terminal. (The terminals are the 1's and 9's of a suit.) May combine with Prevalent Wind or Seat Wind.

74.   Melded Kong   1 point

An exposed kong (whether made by discard or by promoting an exposed pung).

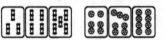

75.   One Voided Suit   1 point

A hand that has tiles from two suits, lacking any tiles of the third suit. Winds or dragons may also be present in the hand.

76.   No Honors   1 point

A hand composed entirely of suit tiles.

77.   Edge Wait   **1 point**

Waiting with an incomplete terminal chow in which the terminal tile and its nearest neighbor are both present, waiting for the missing tile to complete the chow and go mahjong. For example, holding 1 and 2 and waiting for the 3, or holding 9 and 8 and waiting for the 7.

78.   Closed Wait   **1 point**

Card players may think of this as waiting on an "Inside Straight." Holding two tiles separated by a 1-tile gap, waiting for the missing tile to fill the gap, complete the chow, and go mahjong. For example, holding 5 and 7 and waiting for the 6.

79.   Single Wait   **1 point**

Waiting while holding a single tile, waiting for its mate to complete the pair in a typical four-sets-and-a-pair hand.

80.   Self-Drawn   **1 point**

Winning by picking the winning tile from the wall. Also called "self-pick."

81.   Flower Tiles   **1 point**

After winning, each flower or season tile among the winner's melds is worth 1 point. Flowers do not count toward the 8-point minimum score requirement (the hand must be worth 8 points on its own merits, without regard to how many flowers the player has). It is permitted to discard flowers rather than meld them (player must still say "*Hua*"); if the player wins, the discarded flower does not add a point to the score. Winning upon taking a flower replacement earns a point for Self-Drawn only (it does not qualify as Out with Replacement Tile, which is only for kong replacements).

Tallying Score at the Table

When you've won a hand of mahjong, it's your responsibility to add up your score and let the other players know. Because mahjong is played internationally, with players who speak different languages, a system has been developed to illustrate the score tally visually, using tiles from the discard floor. A faceup tile represents 1 point, and a facedown tile represents 10 points.

The player should call out each scoring element that earns points, and line up the corresponding number of discards as he tallies.

For example, the player might say, while pointing to three of his chows, "Mixed Shifted Chows, six points," and line up six faceup discards. Then, waving a hand over the four chows, "All Chows, two points," and bringing two more discards into the lineup.

Eight random discards represents 8 points.

Touching the flowers, "Two flowers, two points." Two more tiles needn't be put in line; now that the tally is 10, one tile is turned facedown and the rest pushed aside: "ten points." The winner then points to the discarder and announces, "eighteen." It's understood that the other players will pay 8.

Chinese players usually do this rapidly (in Chinese, of course), then announce the total as the basic points plus 8 extra points, which can be confusing to new players.

One facedown tile and two faceup represent 12 basic points.

The Chinese player would point to a display of 1 facedown tile and 2 faceup tiles (12 points) and announce, *"Er shuh"* ("twenty"). Everyone knows that the score is the basic points plus 8 basic points. The 8 is assumed (added mentally). Get used to it.

Inclusions & Combinations in Scoring

When scoring a hand, points for numerous scoring elements may be added to arrive at the hand's final score. The rules permit some latitude in this matter, but the rules do prohibit including certain combinations of scoring elements.

The term "set" is used herein to refer to a pung, chow, kong, or pair. In case it helps some readers understand the concept of "sets" in mahjong, consider: most mahjong hands are composed of sets or groupings of tiles. (Exceptions: Thirteen Orphans and the two Knitted and Honors hands, which are composed of particular single tiles rather than sets or groupings of tiles.)

When Scoring a Hand . . .

1. Begin by deciding what is to be your main scoring element (*fan*). The main scoring element of your hand might be the highest-scoring element, typically.

2. Then combine any other scoring elements which are not inevitably included in that main scoring element. One way to look at it is to combine elements in decreasing numbers of sets. In practice, you can usually start by adding any and all scoring elements that use all the sets, all the tiles, or four of the sets (excluding the pair) first. Then you can add two- or three-set scoring elements. Lastly, you would add scoring elements based on concealment and/or how the winning tile had been obtained.

3. Be mindful of the "combine-just-once" principle. Having combined sets to form your main scoring element, any sets not used in that main element may be combined only once, with no more than one set that has already been used to form the main element, to form additional scoring elements. The player is permitted to try differently ordering the combinations to achieve extra points, but it rarely works out that higher scores can be obtained

by doing so. There are other prohibited combinations as well. Examples are given below.

Principles for Scoring the Hand

The scoring of a completed hand is based on the table of scoring elements (*fan*). When a player completes the hand, the player shall identify the primary scoring element first (usually the highest-scoring *fan*), then add other scoring elements that are not inevitably related to, or derived from, the primary scoring element or one another. In calculating the hand's score, the following principles must be observed.

1. **Prohibition Against Implied Inclusions:** When a high-scoring pattern cannot be made without also inevitably making a lesser pattern, you cannot claim both the high-scoring pattern and the inevitable low-scoring pattern. Sometimes referred to as the "nonimplied principle" or the "nonrepeat principle."
2. **Prohibition Against Separation:** Once some sets have been combined to create a particular scoring element, you may not "separate" the tiles of those sets and reorganize them into other sets (or separate the sets of a pattern and reorganize them into other patterns) to form a different scoring element. Sometimes referred to as "unbreakable" or the "nonseparation principle."
3. **Prohibition Against Identical Patterns:** Once you've used a set to form a particular two- or three-set pattern, you can't use the same set to form an identical pattern with another set. Sometimes referred to as the "nonidentical principle."
4. **Freedom of Choice Principle:** If a set can be used to form a low-scoring pattern or a high-scoring pattern, you are free to claim the higher-scoring pattern. Sometimes referred to as the "high-versus-low principle."
5. **Prohibition Against Repetitive Set Usage ("Combine-Just-Once"):** Once two or three sets have been combined for a scoring pattern, any other remaining sets in the hand may be combined only once with an already-scored set, when creating additional two- or three-set scoring patterns. Sometimes referred to as the "exclusionary rule" or the "account-once principle."

Examples

1. **Prohibition Against Implied Inclusions:** When a particular scoring combination cannot possibly be made without also including another (lesser, inevitable) scoring element, the lesser element is said to be "implied"; thus, it is not permitted to combine the two (to add extra points). For instance, the hand All Even Pungs cannot be made with chows or terminals or honors (it can only be made with pungs of even-numbered suit tiles); therefore, it is not permitted to combine the points for All Even Pungs and the points for All Pungs or All Simples or No Honors. All Even Pungs is worth 24 points; the points for those other attributes are "implied" (already included) in the 24 points.

   For another example, it would not be permitted to combine both "half flush" (also called "clean") and "one voided suit."

2. **Prohibition Against Separation:** If you have 111222333 in one suit, you can either call that three pungs or three chows. You can't claim points for calling it chows, then claim additional points for calling it pungs.

3. **Prohibition Against Identical Patterns:** For instance, if you have 123B 456B 456B, you can't say that's two short straights (using the 123B twice to form two identical patterns). Another example.

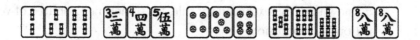

   This hand is All Chows and All Simples. All of the sets in the hand work together, noninevitably, to create these two scoring patterns, and it is permitted to combine them when adding the score.

   In addition, the 234B 345C 456D comprises Mixed Shifted Chows. The winner might wish to claim that the remaining chow, 567B, should be combined with the 345C 456D to make a second Mixed Shifted Chows scoring pattern, but this principle prohibits such a combination, because it uses more than one of the sets in the first Mixed Shifted Chows to make a second Mixed Shifted Chows. However, the 567B can be combined with the 234B to make a Short Straight, because that combination only uses one set from the Mixed Shifted pattern.

Last example:

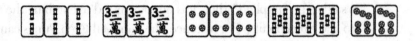

This only earns you Mixed Shifted Pungs once. You cannot take the fourth pung and combine it with two you already "used up" to make a second Mixed Shifted Pungs. To use two sets from the first combination would violate this nonidentical principle. The holder of this hand can take consolation from the fact that this hand is All Pungs (and, if the pair is simples as shown, All Simples).

4. **Freedom of Choice Principle:** For instance, if you have 123 456 789 all in one suit, it makes sense to claim Pure Straight, rather than Short Straight. The Short Straight is inevitable given the Pure Straight. You can't claim both, so claim the more valuable.

   If you can claim Concealed Hand and Self-Drawn (3 points total), it's better to claim Fully Concealed Hand instead (4 points).

5. **Prohibition Against Repetitive Set Usage ("Combine-Just-Once"):** While the above four principles are well understood and accepted by new players, this rule (which has also been known as "the exclusionary rule") is sometimes a source of vexation and confusion.

Consider this Mixed Straight hand:

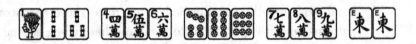

The 123B 456C 789D can be combined to make a Mixed Straight (8 points). That leaves the 789C to be used together with something else in the hand—you can use it just once, *either* to create Short Straight (456789C) *or* to create Mixed Double Chow (789D 789C)—but not both, for an additional point.

Note that in this example, the pair is made of honors. That means the hand does not earn another 2 points for All Chows (more properly, *"Pin Hu"*). There may be other points for the final wait or for concealment.

Also, let's consider an example hand in which numerous two-set patterns may be found.

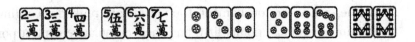

There are several ways the patterns might be combined. All result in the same score.

a. 234C 567C are combined to form a Short Straight. 234D can be combined with 234C to make a Mixed Double Chow. Then the remaining 567D may be combined either with 234D to make a second Short Straight or with 567C to make a second Mixed Double Chow.

b. 234C 234D are combined to form Mixed Double Chow. 567C may be combined with 234C to form a Short Straight. Then the remaining 567D may be combined either with 567C to form a second Mixed Double Chow or with 234D to make a second Short Straight.

c. 234C 567C are combined to form Short Straight. 234D 567D are combined to form a second Short Straight. Because of the wording of the Combine-Just-Once rule, you might be challenged if you then try to use one already-used set with another already-used set to form a Mixed Double Chow. Thus, it might be your best bet to go with A or B instead. Scoring the above hand, you get All Chows (2 points) and All Simples (2), then you can add any three of these four: Mixed Double Chow (1), Mixed Double Chow (1), Short Straight (1), and Short Straight (1). That makes only 7 points—not enough to go out. You'll need to self-pick, go out on a unique wait, keep your hand concealed, or win on the last tile of its kind in order to get at least 1 more point to meet the minimum.

Contest Points & Table Points

At the end of the game session, the player's total points are added to determine the contest points. The player with the highest contest points is the winner of the game, and earns 4 table points for the game session. The player with the second highest score for the game earns 2 table points; the player with the second lowest score for the game earns 1 table point; the lowest-scoring player earns 0 table points.

All in all, there are 7 table points to be apportioned between the players. For example, if two players tie for high score, they both earn 3 table points, and the second-highest scorer earns 1 table point.

At the end of the tournament, the players are ranked according to their cumulative table points first, and their cumulative contest points second. Players whose table points are equal are ranked according to their cumulative contest points. Players with equal table points and contest points share the same ranking for the tournament.

ERRORS & CONFLICTS

Since mahjong players are only human, and odd things can happen, and the rules are sometimes incompletely understood, it's only natural for errors and conflicts to arise. By keeping a cool head, having the rule book handy, and remembering that harmony trumps everything, all can be resolved.

Errors

Some errors incur penalties spelled out in the official rules. If such an error occurs at a tournament, call over a referee to determine whether or not a penalty shall be applied. If an error occurs in the home, the group should abide by the most harmonious means—usually majority consensus. Sometimes it's desirable to loosen the rules for a friendly gathering, and sometimes it's desirable to strictly abide by the official rules in preparation for the actual tournament experience.

Empty Call, Improper Use of Discard

Sometimes a player has a change of heart after verbalizing a call for a discard. This is a no-no in a tournament. The first time a player changes his mind, he gets a warning. The second time, he's docked 5 points; the third time, 10 points, fourth time 20 points, and so on.

When calling for a discard, the player must first expose the tiles from the hand, before taking the discard. He must not first take the discard, put it in the hand, then make the meld. The official rules do not specify the exact penalty for doing this. It could be as minor as docking of points as above, or it could be as major as invalidation of the hand (prohibition from declaring mahjong).

After calling for a discard, it must be taken into the meld before the second subsequent turn. Failure to take the discard disqualifies the hand from winning.

Reaching for the Wall, Touching Wall Too Early

A player who reaches for the wall is not permitted to change his mind and take the most recent discard instead. Taking it invalidates his hand; he must continue playing, but is not permitted to declare mahjong.

A player who touches the wall tile before his upper seat has discarded will be warned the first time, then docked increasing points for each subsequent occurrence as above.

If a player reveals or sees the early-taken tile, he's prohibited from going mahjong.

Late Call, Late Action

A player who wants to pung a discard must say so within 3 seconds from the time the tile was discarded, else be penalized as above. A player who declares chow, pung, or kong on a discard must then act within 2 seconds. Players want to keep the game moving along at a reasonable pace. After exposing tiles from one's hand, the player must take the called discard within a reasonable amount of time. If two turns go by without having taken the discard to put it in the meld, the player is penalized by being prohibited from declaring mahjong.

Wrong Tile Count

A player whose hand is discovered to contain fewer than 13 or more than 13 tiles between turns (fewer than 14 or more than 14 on his turn) is prohibited from declaring mahjong.

False Mahjong

A player who declares mahjong with an invalid hand is penalized according to the nature of the exact error. The penalty is normally 10 points to each opponent for calling mahjong with a ready hand, and 20 points to each opponent for calling mahjong with a hand that is not yet ready.

The player is disqualified from winning the current hand after making false mahjong.

A player who declares mahjong but later is found to have a hand worth fewer than 8 points is penalized 10 points to each opponent and is disqualified from making mahjong for the remainder of the current hand.

A player who exposes the tiles in the course of making false mahjong is penalized for the false claim, but is not penalized for exposure (the player is not required to discard all exposed tiles, as is done with erroneous exposure as outlined below).

When disqualified from winning, the player continues playing normally. He may pick and discard, and call for exposures. It's wise to play defensively in such a case.

Errors in Declaring Mahjong

In declaring mahjong, a player must (1) say *"Hu,"* (2) expose the hand, (3) put the winning tile with the hand but placed apart, and (4) tally the hand's value using discards. Failure to follow the correct procedure is a punishable error.

After the player has declared mahjong by discard, the player must take the discard into the exposed hand before starting to count the points. Failure to do this is regarded as False Mahjong. The player pays a penalty of 10 points to each opponent and is disqualified from winning the current hand.

If declaring mahjong by discard, the player is only permitted to say *"Hu"* (or "Mahjong")—the player is not allowed to say "Chow" or "Pung" or "Kong" first, before saying *"Hu."* The player who commits this error must discard a tile, and is permitted to win on a subsequent go-around if possible.

A player who says *"Hu"* but does not expose the tiles ("Empty *Hu*") is disqualified only from winning the current hand. There is no points penalty.

When tallying one's points, only discarded tiles may be used to display the tally. If the player includes any tiles from his own hand in the tally display, his win is declared invalid, and he is penalized 10 points per opponent.

Upon declaring mahjong, a player must tally his score and have it validated by the others (and by an umpire, if one is at hand). The player is not permitted to claim more points than the hand is actually worth, but if the player claims fewer points than the hand is worth, he won't be corrected. If anybody asks you "Are you sure?" that probably means you can claim more than you have.

A player who is unable to tally the score may be penalized by having the hand valued at the minimum 8 points, provided that the hand is worth at least that much.

Exposed Tile(s)

If a player accidentally or erroneously exposes one of his own tiles, then on his next turn he is required to discard that tile. If a player accidentally exposes an opponent's tile, he pays the player 5 points for each tile exposed. In a tournament, the referee may also impose a prohibition against declaring mahjong.

If a player exposes his hand because another player has declared mahjong, the exposed player's penalty depends on whether or not the player who declared mahjong won with a valid hand. If the other player's hand is declared valid, the exposed player is warned. If the other player's hand is declared invalid, the exposed player must upright his tiles and discard them one by one during the course of play, and is prohibited from declaring mahjong, and must pay 10 points to each opponent (a total of 30 points).

There is no penalty for accidentally knocking a tile off the wall and revealing it. It's polite to apologize when this happens.

Other Errors

A player who exposes a set with incorrect tiles (such as mistaking a flower for a One Bam) is required to leave the incorrect set as is, and may not declare mahjong. When a One Bam is mistakenly melded as a flower, it may be taken by another player for mahjong if it is the last One Bam (Last Tile is awarded).

There may also be other errors, not covered above or in the official rules. In a home game with no official umpires, players should use common sense to determine the reasonable penalty, be it warnings, docking of points, or invalidation of the hand.

In a tournament, when an error or question comes up, the referee or umpire should be consulted immediately. Once the game has moved on, there can be no retroactive judgment.

Appeals

In a tournament, players may appeal punitive rulings made against them. Such appeals must be made immediately or within a very short time. To prevent frivolous appeals, the official judges will require that a fee be paid on the spot when the appeal is submitted in writing. The fee is returned if the appealing player is vindicated.

Resolving Conflicts

The official rules describe specific penalties for specific errors. But sometimes unexpected situations may arise, in which one player believes he or she has been wronged by another player's action, whether or not either one's action is explicitly covered by the rules. See Appendix 4 for some philosophies that may help resolve such situations.

Etiquette

It can't be overstated: harmony is very important in mahjong. Above all, avoid actions or noises that disrupt the game.

Talking, Making Noise

Don't clack your tiles together between turns, and don't carry on a conversation while playing. Don't fidget. During a tournament, talking is frowned upon. You may see others do it a little, but unless it's excessive or disturbing to your concentration, let it slide, and don't do it yourself. There is a strict penalty for giving game information during a tournament, whether or not the information is used by another player to his own advantage.

Verbal Calls

Players are required to speak when calling for a discard, when exposing a flower, when declaring mahjong, and when tallying the score. When taking a discard, the player can only say what the tile is being taken for: "*Chi*" (when making a chow), "pung," "kong," "*Hwar*" (when exposing a flower). The American practice of saying simply, "I want that," or "Call," is forbidden. And it's not necessary or allowed to speak the name of a tile when discarding it. If you can learn to announce the value of the hand in Chinese, you'll win new friends.

Keep It Moving

Every player has his own rhythm; not everybody plays at the same speed. Don't be the slowest player at the table, or if you are, do your best to keep up. During the deal, if other players are examining their tiles (rather than waiting until the deal is complete), you should do the same. Pay attention, and act when you're expected to act. Go with the flow.

Neatness Counts

Some players are careless about organizing their melds and discards. Don't be one of them. Your discards should form a reasonably neat row, arranged chronologically from left to right, and after a row is six tiles long, the next row should go beneath it (nearer you than the previous row). Your melds should be placed between your hand and your discards. It makes it easier for everyone to read the table.

Superstition

The Chinese are famous for having a variety of popular superstitions. The most important one you need to know as a mahjong player is that you must never discard the fourth West Wind tile in succession. It's said that when four wests are discarded in rapid succession, someone will die. This is because of the similarity between the way "West" and "Death" are pronounced in Chinese. So if the three players before you discard west, one after the other, and you are holding the fourth one and wish to discard it, hold it until your next turn, when it'll be acceptable to throw it.

Danish player Henrik Leth has his own take on superstition in mahjong. He says: "It brings bad luck to be superstitious."

C. Strategy for Chinese Official Mahjong

Mahjong strategy takes many forms. The primary strategies for building the hand consist of choosing which tiles to discard and which discarded tiles to claim. But there are also defensive strategies, in which the player keeps an eye on other players' discards and exposures and body language, as well as an eye on the wall as it diminishes. Different types of Chinese Official hands even have their own strategies.

Although Chinese Official and other Asian forms of mahjong are easy to learn, mastering the strategy provides a fascinating challenge that can last a lifetime.

CHANCE VS. SKILL

British playing card author David Parlett speaks of the difference between "luck" and "chance." The word "luck" too often conjures the image in the listener's mind of good luck, whereas "chance" is less connotative one way or the other. In Monopoly, they don't call 'em "Luck Cards," after all.

There is no way to derive a measurable way of defining how much of mahjong is chance, and how much of it is skill. Chance vs. skill in mahjong is probably best understood another way. An unskilled beginner may occasionally chance upon a lucky set of tiles and circumstances and win a hand, or even prevail one lucky evening. But in the long run, the skilled player will win more often with higher scores. These skills can be learned. It can be argued that mahjong is more a game of skill than of chance.

1. BASIC MAHJONG STRATEGY (ALL ASIAN FORMS)

If you are a raw beginner and have never played any form of mahjong before, this section will help get you started. These are basic strategies that players of Chinese Official mahjong use, but these principles won't make you a master Chinese Official player in and of themselves. One way to start out learning is to play a computer mahjong game that permits the player to make cheap hands, playing according to Chinese Classical, Hong Kong Old Style, or even Japanese *Riichi/Dora Majan*. Playing such a computer game, the novice can learn much basic strategy that will be useful in playing the Chinese Official game.

The basic principles beginners need to study first are connectedness, calling patterns, patience, defense, body language, and the three stages of a mahjong hand.

Connectedness

The concept of connectedness is basic to the building of a complete hand of mahjong, in all forms of the game. It's the first strategy that must be learned.

In the basic beginner strategy of connectedness (while playing practice hands not involving scoring), one simply discards tiles that are not "connected" to other tiles in the hand.

The typical mahjong hand consists of "four groups and a pair," in which a "group" is usually either a pung (3 identical tiles) or a chow (a run of 3 sequential numbered tiles in the same suit). Thus, the following types of tiles can be considered as being "connected":

Two identical tiles.

Two identical tiles can be either kept as a pair, or if one adds another, the twosome can be turned into a pung. In terms of connectedness, a pair of identical tiles is clearly a very strong connection. Sometimes a player will be waiting for mahjong with two pairs in the hand (and waiting for a tile to turn one of them into a pung). A two-way call is clearly better than a one-way call.

Two sequential same-suit tiles.

Two same-suit sequential tiles form an incomplete chow, with a two-way call. In this example, a 4 and 5 of Dots, the player can call either a 3 or a 6. In terms of connectedness, a two-number same-suit sequence like this is clearly a very strong connection.

Same-suit tiles separated by one number.

Two same-suit tiles separated by one number form an incomplete chow, with a one-way call (in cards the term is "filling an inside straight"). In this example, a 2 and 4 of Bams, the player can only call a Three. In terms of connectedness, a one-way incomplete chow like this is pretty weakly connected. Consider also the one-way terminal chow.

Two one-way incomplete terminal chows.

Holding a 1 and a 2, without the 3, or holding an 8 and a 9, without the 7, is a one-way incomplete chow. There's only one way to complete the chow, making it a weak connection.

Calling Patterns

The basic principle of connectedness goes well beyond the simple 2-tile patterns discussed above, to include incomplete patterns of larger numbers of tiles. When the hand is nearly complete, an understanding of these basic calling patterns are of enormous help to the strategic mahjong player.

Imagine that you are playing a hand composed of three complete sets and two pairs. Imagine that if the hand is completed, it meets the score requirements. Your hand is complete except for the two pairs shown in this figure.

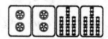

Not bad, you think. A two-way call (2D, 7B). But then on your next turn, you pick 6B. Ignoring complications of scoring for a moment, which tile do you discard now? In this situation, many experienced players will discard a 7B, keeping 6B 7B. This is a better two-way call, because there are more possible tiles with which you can win. It's a matter of the odds of getting a tile you need. If you are holding two pairs and waiting to pung one, there are just 4 tiles out of the entire 144 tiles that you can use. But if you have 2 sequential tiles waiting to chow, there are 8 tiles you can use. Double the chances.

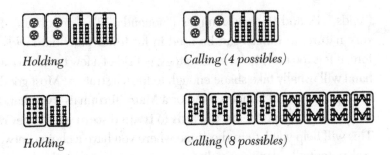

Holding *Calling (4 possibles)*

Holding *Calling (8 possibles)*

Clearly, the two-ended chow wait is more powerful than the two-pair call.

5-tile same-suit sequence.

With a 5-tile same-suit sequence such as this example, assuming the rest of the hand is complete, the player has a three-way call (any of 3 tiles will give the calling player mahjong). The player is waiting for 1, 4, or 7 of Dots. With a 5-tile sequence, the player is always waiting for either 1-4-7 or 2-5-8 or 3-6-9. When the rest of the hand is complete, the three-way call is clearly a very powerful position in which to be. Similarly, it's wise to learn to shape the hand into calling patterns that give you multiple chances to win, such as the following:

Holding	Calling
23456	147
34567	258
45678	369
4445	356
4446	56
4445566	4567
4445556	4567
4445678	36958
44456EE	47E

In considering the various calling patterns involved in chow hands, it's important to keep in mind the profound difference between terminals ("ends," 1's and 9's) and simples ("nonends," 2's through 8's). By their very nature, terminals can be used in far fewer potential melds. Therefore, if it is too early to form a strategy, get rid of a few terminals, and your hand will usually take shape enough to form a strategy. Most good players often go for an All Simples hand or a Many Terminals–type hand—keep an eye on your opponents' discards to try to discern which they're doing. This will help you late in the game where you have a choice between several potentially dangerous discards—remember that the terminals are usually in less demand. Most one-way calling hands are not waiting for terminals.

Patience

Don't grab the first discard that completes one of your sets. Many beginners think that making melds (chows pungs, kongs) is a good thing, because it means they are making good progress in completing the hand. But what they don't realize is that melding is an onerous duty, not a sign of success! If you watch experienced players, you will see that they do not necessarily grab the first tile that comes along. For one thing, melding shows the other players 3 tiles that you have collected; opponents can learn more about your hand by the melds and discards than they could from the discards alone. But more important, melding narrows the opportunities for the hand you are building. A meld cannot be taken back. Once a meld is made, you've committed your hand in a particular direction, whether you come to regret it or not. Besides, a concealed hand earns more points. The value of a hand can be reduced by making an unwise meld. In general, don't take somebody else's discard unless you have a clear plan for your hand and that discard advances the hand closer to a win.

Keep a pair. It's harder to make a pair if you have only 1 tile than it is to make a pung if you have a pair. So if you have a pair, don't be too quick to claim a matching tile to form a pung.

Flexibility

Mahjong players must be flexible. As you build your hand, be ready to abandon your earlier thinking about how to build it as you see what kind of tiles others are discarding. The strategic player preserves multiple options for the hand as long as possible, then when one becomes stronger, or a new and stronger option arises, works toward that stronger option.

DEFENSIVE BASICS

Try not to let someone else win. As much as you want to go out yourself, sometimes it's wiser to keep anybody else from winning. Especially, you don't want to feed a high-scoring hand. If a player has melded three sets of all one suit, for example, then you shouldn't discard other tiles of that same suit, if you can avoid it.

Watch the discards and watch the number of tiles in the wall. As it approaches the end, the tension increases—and it's more important to be careful what you discard when there are fewer tiles remaining to be drawn. If the number of tiles in the wall is getting low, don't discard any tiles whose mates are not visible among the discards or exposures.

Body Language

Develop a Poker Face (or "Poker Body Language"). Experienced players hardly ever look up from their tiles, much less look up to see the expressions on each other's faces. But body movements and postures can be seen out the corner of one's eye (via peripheral vision).

Even alterations in the speed of discarding can give experienced players clues about what you're doing. If you pick a tile, study it, then reluctantly discard it, they can tell that it's a tile you might have a use for, and that gives them information about your hand. It's wise to do your thinking before picking, and have a tile ready to discard. Then when you pick, just discard your prechosen tile.

Subtle subterfuge can be used as well. Picking and discarding several tiles in a row, then keeping one with a determined gesture, can make someone think you just became ready for mahjong. If the other players think you are waiting, they will become more cautious, and may even give up their own hands to play defensively.

Another sort of subterfuge is to treat every pick the same—don't react differently, don't think longer. And watch the other players for subtle unconscious signals they may be sending.

THE THREE STAGES OF A MAHJONG HAND

Your strategy must go through three stages or phases throughout the play of each hand. Each stage is characterized by a different activity.

Stage	Characteristic
1. Opening	Develop
2. Middle game	Attack
3. End game	Defend

Stage 1: Opening

The first stage of the game moves quickly, as the players remove unconnected tiles from their hands.

When you get your dealt tiles, first evaluate the potential of your hand. If you have a lot of pairs, plan to try for an All Pairs hand or an All Pung hand. Determine as early as possible what hand you think you can get. Consider whether you want to throw away terminals or simples, whether to keep or discard honors, whether to go for chows or pungs or pairs or a special hand. Keep your options open; much depends on what you draw.

In this stage, you shouldn't take somebody else's discard unless you have a clear plan for your hand and that discard advances the hand closer to a win.

Be mindful of your wind and the prevailing wind. It's usual to hang on to those particular wind tiles in the early part of a hand until the player can see that they're hopeless or that the hand is shaping another way. On the other hand, your own wind (when it's not the round wind) may well be safe to discard.

If a pair of dragons has already been thrown, the third and fourth tile of that same dragon tile are probably safe to discard.

This first stage of the game lasts no longer than the first eight turns (when all players are showing eight discards: one row of six, plus two tiles in the second row).

Stage 2: Middle Game

Things don't move quite so quickly anymore, once all the players have zeroed in on their hands and are watching for opportunities to take discards to further the hand toward the goal.

In this stage, it's important to be flexible. If the plan you'd been working on in stage one is not working, you have to be prepared to switch plans. It's quite possible that someone will go out during this stage.

Stage 3: Endgame

In the third stage, several of the players are nearing mahjong. It's a dangerous stage, during which someone could win at any time. Things slow down in this stage, as players carefully consider what should and should not be discarded. Try to balance safety against your desire to win. If you give someone else a win, your own beautiful tiles (so carefully collected and built) will be useless. There can be only one winner in mahjong.

Know what's safe to discard. Watch the discards and don't discard any tiles that are not visible among the discards and exposures. If you pick flowers, you may discard them rather than meld them.

2. BASIC STRATEGY FOR CHINESE OFFICIAL MAHJONG

For those who've learned the mahjong basics and who are getting started with the Chinese Official game, basic strategy consists of three parts: pattern familiarization, multiple options, and beginner target hands.

Patterns

Chinese Official mahjong is a pattern-based game. The types of patterns fall into these main types:

- Honors
- Chows
- Pungs and Kongs
- Seven Pairs
- Suits
- Terminals
- Knitted
- Types of Waits
- Special

Let's examine each type of pattern with an eye to strategy.

Honor-based and suit-based hands fall into two different types of patterns: all of a particular kind of tile, and none of that kind of tile. For example:

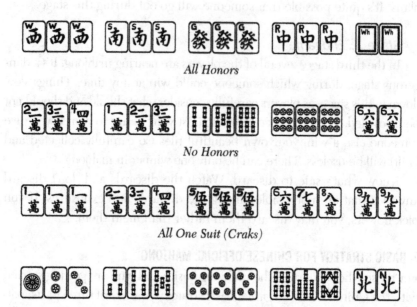

All Honors

No Honors

All One Suit (Craks)

One Voided Suit (no Craks)

There are honor-based *fan* that involve the entire hand (such as All Honors) or only four sets (such as Big Four Winds or Little Four Winds), and even some that involve only one set (Prevalent Wind, Dragon Pung).

Chow-based hands are the biggest category, divided into several subcategories: shifted chows, same-sequence chows, straights, and terminal chows (chows that contain a terminal tile).

Pung-based *fan* include kongs. Remember that a kong is nothing more than a glorified pung. Two of the categories include just two *fan* each: the seven pairs category and the knitted tiles category. The "special" category includes *fan* that don't fit into the other categories.

It behooves the player to familiarize himself with the various patterns represented in the 81 *fan*, and learn to use this familiarity strategically. Patterns are not just to make the game pretty or interesting—they are the way to get high score.

Multiple Options

Only occasionally, the tiles the player is dealt clearly indicate one particular hand, and no other. Most of the time, the tiles are enigmatic, suggesting several different possibilities, or none at all. The strategic player works to nourish and develop those multiple options until a clear direction makes itself evident.

In the example above, the player might want to develop the hand in several different ways: Mixed Straight (123 in Dots, 456 in Craks, 789 in Bams), or Mixed Shifted Chows (345 in Dots, 456 in Craks, 567 in Bams). The player might even try to make a Pure Straight in Dots. By choosing to discard a tile that does not ruin one of his target hands, the player can possibly draw a tile that gives him a clear direction. In this example, discarding 6B preserves all the options (but leaves the hand without a pair).

Having serendipitously added 7B to the hand, it's now clear to the player that he can go for Mixed Shifted Chows and All Chows, to make the minimum 8-point requirement. If he desires, he can now discard 1D and possibly add All Simples to the mix.

Beginner Target Hands

When starting to learn the Chinese Official game, most players find themselves daunted by the long list of scoring elements. Eighty-one *fan* seems like a lot to absorb all at once. For most people starting out, it may be best to focus on a few types of target hands. The repertoire can be expanded later, with experience at playing the official game. For starters, memorize a few 8-point, 6-point, and 2-point *fan*.

8-Point Fan

When the player is shooting for an 8-point *fan*, there need be no worrying about how to make the minimum 8 points. The most common 8-point *fan* to memorize are:

Mixed Triple Chow
Mixed Straight
Reversible

The problem with going for 8-point *fan* is that they aren't easy! It's easier to go for a 6-point *fan*, to which you also have to add a 2-point *fan* (or two 1-point *fan*).

6-Point Fan

You can earn 6 points with some easier patterns. Then you only need to add 2 more points to make the 8-point minimum requirement. The most common 6-point *fan* the beginner should memorize are:

Mixed Shifted Chows
All Pungs
All Types
Half Flush (also called "clean" or "semipure")

2-Point Fan

Adding 2 more points is not very difficult. You can add two 1-point *fan*, but it may be easier for a beginner simply to memorize the most common 2-point *fan*:

Dragon Pung
Prevalent Wind
Seat Wind
All Chows
All Simples

Now you have a perfectly workable beginner repertoire.

3. ADVANCED STRATEGY

Once you've mastered basic mahjong strategy and the most common beginner Chinese Official *fan,* you're ready for advanced strategy.

The Power of Mixed Shifted Chows

Two of the top Japanese players in the international circuit, Mai Hatsune (champion at the first World Mahjong Championship in 2002) and Takunori Kajimoto, swear by Mixed Shifted Chows as the king of the *fan.* The reason why this hand is favored? It's extremely flexible.

Chows are the easiest type of set to make in mahjong, because there are four of each numbered tile in a suit. Mixed Shifted Chows in particular offers even more possibilities, for reasons that are too mathematical for this author to describe.

When you have a hodgepodge of suit tiles, some judicious discarding of outer tiles can be used to shift the focus of one suit toward the focus of the other suits. Develop this practice and you'll see its power. This practice, and the usual practice of discarding disconnected terminals, makes it challenging to balance a Straight option with a Mixed Shifted Chows option. When faced with a choice between the two, unless the tiles predominate toward the Straight, remember the power of Mixed Shifted Chows.

Not Everything Can Always Be Mixed Shifted Chows

While Mixed Shifted Chows is highly useful, sometimes the tiles suggest a different direction. Numbered suit tiles separated by two numbers from one another suggest a possible Knitted hand. Honors and terminals likewise offer nonchow possibilities.

And don't forget those reversible tiles. When using tiles marked with Western indices, one can lose sight of the fact that some of the tiles can be turned upside down. The player who learns to recognize the winds and Craks without need for the Western indices gives himself a big advantage over players who rely on the indices to read the tiles. And if you play in China or Japan, the tiles may not have indices at all.

While we're on the subject of reading the tiles, a simple computer game can be helpful. It's easy to find free mahjong tile-matching games on the Internet. Playing these games is good practice. The eye becomes accustomed to searching for a particular tile among a pile of other tiles, a useful skill when playing a game of mahjong.

All Rules Were Meant to Be Broken

The most skilled strategists are very familiar with these and other "rules" of strategy, so that the rules can be broken properly. Sometimes you're "in the zone," you have a dream hand, and you can smell victory just around the corner. When this happens, forget the usual rules, and just go for it.

Steve Sera, a skilled player of Japanese mahjong in Los Angeles, once told me that his strategy is to "know who has the luck. When *you* have it, attack!"

Challenging for a Lifetime

The strategies outlined above just scratch the surface. As you play, you will discover other strategies of your own. You'll discover the importance of knowing the standing score, in order to know which opponent to attack. You'll see for yourself the value of keeping flexible, even when you are just one tile away from mahjong. Mahjong strategy is rich enough and deep enough to challenge you for a long, happy, and active life.

APPENDIX 1
Where to Buy a Mah-Jongg Set, & What Not to Buy

Today, the easiest place to find a variety of mah-jongg sets is on the Internet. If you live in a large city with a Chinatown district, you can find mah-jongg sets for sale there. If you live in such a city, just go on a shopping adventure. And make sure to have some Chinese food while you're there.

On the Internet, some of the most well-known vendors' sites in North America are:

- http://nationalmahjonggleague.org
- http://www.kmaindustries.com
- http://www.wherethewindsblow.com
- http://exclusivelymahjongg.com
- http://amja.net
- http://www.mahjonggmaven.com

In Europe:

- http://www.dajamahjong.nl
- http://www.donaygames.com

And more links to mah-jongg vendors may be found on the author's Web site at:

- http://www.sloperama.com/majexchange/links.htm
- http://www.sloperama.com/mjfaq/mjfaq04.htm

When buying a mah-jongg set, you must make sure that the set is suitable for the kind of mah-jongg you want to use it for.

What to Buy If You Play American Mah-Jongg

You have to have at least 152 tiles to play American mah-jongg. You must *not* purchase a Chinese set, if you want to play American mah-jongg with it. Or if you do buy a Chinese set, buy two. That way you have enough extra tiles so you can make jokers. Joker stickers are available from several online vendors. You can sell the remaining tiles to crafts people who use them to make picture frames, bookends, and other tchotchkes.

Also if you play American mah-jongg, make sure that the tiles have indices in the corners of the tiles. Your friends can't read Chinese, so they'd have trouble with the Craks and winds, if you don't get a set with indices.

American players expect to use racks to hold the tiles, to line up the walls, and to display exposed melds. Make sure the set you buy comes with racks and dice.

Most American sets also come with chips, but most American players play for coins (and do not use the chips).

What to Buy If You Play Chinese Official Mahjong

Any kind of mahjong set is suitable for the Chinese Official game. An American set is perfectly fine; just leave the jokers in the carrying case.

Most players of Chinese Official mahjong do not use racks. The customary practice instead is to stand the tiles on end. If you want something more Chinese-style than an American set (one with Chinese characters on the dragon tiles, rather than depictions of dragons, or one without indices, or one with larger tiles), there are a large variety of Asian sets available. Just be sure whether or not you need the indices. Maybe *you* can read the Craks and winds, but maybe your friends cannot.

Most Chinese sets come with dice, but most Chinese dice are very small. You can get bigger dice at the corner drugstore (next to the playing cards).

Some people believe that bone and bamboo tiles are more "authentic," but as a general rule, plastic tiles are better on many counts. They're usually more square, which means they stack better. They're usually bigger, which means they're easier to read and to handle. It's not difficult to find attractive plastic tiles. Don't be a slave to uninformed preconceived notions.

Even bigger tiles (such as those favored in China today) may be even better. They're easier to read, but they're heavier to schlep around.

APPENDIX 2
How to Order a Card for American Mah-Jongg

The National Mah Jongg League has been the governing body for American mah-jongg since 1937. Other cards come and go, but the NMJL card is and always has been the standard card used by American players.

The NMJL card can be ordered from Internet mah-jongg merchandise sellers, and some groups purchase cards in bulk for their members. But it is *strongly* recommended that you purchase it directly from the league. When you purchase the card directly from the league, you are added to their mailing list. Then, each January, the yearly NMJL bulletin will be mailed directly to you. The bulletin is very important. Each year, new rule refinements are announced in the bulletin. It's smart to keep the bulletins in order to stay on top of the rule changes. The NMJL card can be obtained from:

NATIONAL MAH JONGG LEAGUE
250 West 57th Street
New York, NY 10107
Phone: 212-246-3052
Fax: 212-246-4117
Web site: http://nationalmahjonggleague.org/

The NMJL card alternates between red and blue each year. In 2006 it was red. The 2007 card should be blue. The NMJL offers both a regular-size card and a larger card for those whose vision needs that extra little help. The NMJL card is updated every year and is mailed out at the end of March of that year (the players receive the new card on or about April 1).

APPENDIX 3

Playing Mah-Jongg on the Computer & on the Internet

For those who enjoy mah-jongg and who have a computer, it's only right and natural to want to play mah-jongg on the computer. It's a way to play more often than one can get together with other nearby players, and it's a way to practice and enhance one's skills.

There are two distinctly different types of mah-jongg programs (real mah-jongg versus tile-matching games), and there are two distinctly different ways to play (off-line versus online).

Real Mah-Jongg Games vs. Solitaire Tile-Matching Games

The first computer game to use graphic representations of mah-jongg tiles was Shanghai, published for the Apple Macintosh computer by Activision in 1986. A simple solitaire tile-matching game played with stacked mah-jongg tiles, it was a big hit that spawned a world of copycats and spinoffs. Activision created and licensed several new versions of Shanghai on numerous video-game and computer platforms worldwide, especially in Japan. Although Activision stopped making new Shanghai games in 2000, a number of similar, free, and downloadable programs are available today on the Internet. It's easy to find them: just search for the keywords "mahjong game" or "mah-jongg download" or any variation thereof. The authors of these Shanghai copycat programs either don't know that mah-jongg is not a tile-matching game, or they don't care, because the use of the name is the means by which they get people to download their games.

221

Tile-matching games, even though they aren't really mah-jongg, are very useful as training aids for beginning players . . . and they're fun, too. These games train the player to spot any tile among a jumble of other tiles; a useful skill when playing the actual game. This author recommends playing tile-matching games to all players. A list of tile-matching programs is available on the author's Web site, at http://www.sloperama.com/mjfaq/mjfaq12.htm.

Real mah-jongg games are also available in abundance. The first successful real mah-jongg computer game was Hong Kong Mahjong Pro, published by Electronic Arts in 1992 (developed by Nine Dragons Software). As might be guessed from the game's title, the game supported the Hong Kong Old Style rules.

When searching for real mah-jongg games online today, one will find programs supporting a variety of regional variants, usually Chinese Classical or Hong Kong Old Style. For those who can read Japanese, there is a plethora of Japanese programs out there. An important computer game available at the time of this writing is Four Winds, by Lagarto. The game supports a variety of variants, including the Chinese Official rules. A comprehensive list of mah-jongg programs (online and off-line) is available on the author's Web site, at http://www.sloperama.com/mjfaq/mjfaq05.htm.

Online vs. Off-line Play

It's important to understand the difference between online play and off-line play. When playing online, one is playing over the Internet, against other real people. When playing off-line, one is playing against computerized opponents, at one's own pace.

When playing online against other people, there are aspects of pressure and etiquette to consider. The other people want the game to move quickly, and if you move too slowly, they may ostracize you or even "boot" you (meaning they kick you off the table so they can find someone faster).

When playing off-line against computerized opponents, the challenge is reduced, but nobody can complain if you get distracted by the telephone or your spouse or your pet or the television.

Limited Choices

At the time of this writing, there are only two choices for those wishing to play American mah-jongg on the computer. The National Mah Jongg League program (available for subscription from the league's Web site, http://national

mahjonggleague.org/), is the primary online game. Mahjong Time (www .mahjongtime.com) has newly created an American mode, but players are hard to find. Both are playable online only.

At the time of this writing, there are a couple of off-line versions of the Chinese Official game:

- Four Winds—http://www.4windsmj.com/
- Chinese Official Mahjong—http://www.ninedragons.com/mahjong/comj .html

And some online mah-jongg sites are starting to offer the Chinese Official game as well. For instance:

- Mahjong Time—http://www.mahjongtime.com/
- Mahjong Mania—http://www.mahjongmania.com/
- Jade Dragon—http://www.jadedragonmahjong.com/

APPENDIX 4
General Principles for Resolving Disagreements or Errors

- When an error affects the erring player's own hand only, and it can be undone without harm to anyone, he or she may retract the move so long as the rules do not say otherwise.
- When an error is discovered too late (after making a move that closes the window of opportunity to rectify the error), then it cannot be undone, and the erring player must accept the consequences.
- When an error affects the entire game, and it's realized immediately, then it must be undone immediately, as long as the rules permit.
- When an error affects the entire game, and it is realized too late (after subsequent moves have cemented the error), it may be best for all players to throw in their hands and start over. A penalty to the erring player(s) may apply.
- When a conflict arises from someone's error, first determine who made the error. It sometimes occurs that one error is compounded by another. The initiating error may be the sole responsibility of one player, but other players who erred as a result may not be immune from the consequences.
- When a conflict cannot be resolved without perpetrating a perceived unfairness on someone, seek the smallest unfairness to the smallest number of players.
- If you make a mistake, you are the one who should suffer its consequences, not everybody else at the table. You can ask to undo it, but there is no rule that says mistakes must be forgiven by the other players.

- Harmony is more important than winning. If a conflict was ruled against you, or if your request for a chance to do something over was turned down, or if you had to throw in a potentially great hand because of someone else's error, then accept it graciously and move on. And no grousing about it later. If all you care about is winning, nobody will want to play with you. Good gamesmanship is about much more than just winning. It's about getting along, too.
- Not only is it important to lose graciously, it's also important to win graciously. Don't be too smug when you're on a roll. Compliment others when they win or make a good move.
- When playing with a new group, be flexible. Find out what table rules they use. Conversely, if someone new joins your table, tell her about your table rules before beginning play.

APPENDIX 5
Other Popular Mahjong Variants

The most popular other variants of mahjong are Hong Kong Old Style, Japanese *Riichi/Dora Majan*, Western Style, and Wright-Patterson. Also worth mentioning are Taiwanese, Filipino, Vietnamese, and Chinese Classical. There are twenty other variants beyond the above and the two variants discussed in this book, but the ones listed here are the most popular.

1. Hong Kong Old Style (Cantonese)
   a. One of the most basic, simplest forms of the game. Was probably created as a simplified variant to fix the complicated scoring of Chinese Classical.
   b. Uses 136 or 144 tiles. Flowers are optional; if used, they are melded instantly when received.
   c. Hold 13 tiles in the hand, go out on 14 tiles.
   d. Small number of special hands.
   e. Score by counting doubles (*fan*), then convert to points.
   f. Only the winner is paid.

2. Japanese *Riichi/Dora Majan*
   a. Uses 136 tiles. Flowers come with the tile sets, but are not used in play.
   b. Many players use red 5's. One 5 tile of each suit is specially colored, and earns double score for the winner whose hand contains such a tile.

c. Hold 13 tiles in the hand, go out on 14 tiles.

d. Many special scoring elements (*yaku*).

e. Score most easily by memorizing chart. Base points times doubles (*fan*).

f. Only the winner is paid. There may be multiple winners (discarder pays all winners).

3. Western Style

a. This form of mahjong is referred to by some authors as "American," but it's most widely played in English-speaking countries other than the United States. Alternative appropriate names for this variant might be "English Style" or "British Style."

b. Uses 144 or more tiles. Jokers are optional and may vary in number. Flowers are melded instantly when received.

c. Hold 13 tiles in the hand, go out on 14 tiles.

d. Many special hands (70 to 80 scoring elements) which vary slightly from book to book.

e. Score 20 points for mahjong, then count up points based on pungs, kongs, and pairs, then double.

f. All players earn points (not only the winner).

4. Wright-Patterson

a. An offshoot of Western Style mahjong, created to serve wives of U.S. military officers who had to deal with multiple variants played in various locales where officers and their wives might be stationed. Governed by a committee of the Officers Wives Club of the Wright-Patterson Air Force Base in Ohio.

b. Uses 144 tiles. Flowers are melded instantly when received.

c. Hold 13 tiles in the hand, go out on 14 tiles.

d. Many special hands (70 to 80 scoring elements).

e. Count up points based on pungs, kongs, and pairs, then double.

f. All players earn points (not only the winner).

5. Taiwanese

a. Uses 144 tiles. Flowers are melded instantly when received.

b. Hold 16 tiles in the hand, go out on 17 tiles.

c. Several special hands (scoring elements).

d. Score by counting doubles (*tai*), then convert to points.

e. Only the winner is paid.

6. Filipino
   a. Uses 144 tiles. Certain tiles in the set may be designated as jokers per game circumstances. Flowers are melded instantly when received; winds and dragons are treated the same as flowers.
   b. Hold 16 tiles in the hand, go out on 17 tiles.
   c. Several special hands (scoring elements). Kongs earn payment instantly when melded.
   d. Score by counting doubles, then convert to points.
   e. Only the winner is paid; discarder pays double.

7. Vietnamese
   a. Uses 160 or 176 tiles.
   b. Includes 8 flowers/seasons, 8 kings/queens, and 8 or 24 jokers (classic game uses 8 jokers; modern game uses 24 jokers).
   c. There are nineteen ways to win (scoring elements).
   d. Scoring is based on the nineteen scoring elements.
   e. Only the winner is paid.

8. Chinese Classical
   a. First popularized in the 1920s.
   b. Uses 144 tiles.
   c. Flowers are melded instantly when received.
   d. Hold 13 tiles in the hand, go out on 14 tiles.
   e. Not many special hands (approximately nineteen scoring elements).
   f. Score 10 or 20 points for mahjong, then add points for valuable pungs, kongs, and pairs, then double per scoring elements earned.
   g. All players earn points (not only the winner).

APPENDIX 6
Glossary of Mahjong Terms

All Green—A Chinese Official hand composed of nothing but bamboo tiles that don't use any red, blue, or black paint (disregarding the indices), specifically the 2, 3, 4, 6, and 8 of bamboo. Green Dragons may also optionally be included.

American Mah-Jongg—A unique variant of mahjong in which players are permitted only to make hands listed on a card that changes yearly, utilizing a set of 152 tiles (the standard set plus 8 jokers). Chows are not used in American mah-jongg, and flowers are used to form sets in the hand. Played primarily by women. Governed by the National Mah Jongg League since 1937.

Animal Tiles—A type of flower tile depicting animals, people, or objects (rather than flowers).

Announcing—The practice of saying the name of the tile being discarded. Not used in Asia.

Any—American game. A word used often in parentheticals on the card, to advise the player that not only the suit, number, or specific tile shown may be used, regardless of the color-coding on the card. Defined herein because of frequent questions.

Any Three Suits—A phrase used in parentheticals on the American card, to advise the player that the color-coding shown on the card does not dictate a particular suit.

Any Consecutive Run—A phrase used in parentheticals on the American card, to advise the player that the numbers shown on the card do not dictate particular numbers.

Any Dragon—A phrase used in parentheticals on the American card, to advise the player that the color-coding shown on the card does not dictate a dragon of a particular suit.

Atomic—A table rule used by some American players in which a player may make a hand of random pairs, provided that the player never had a joker. Rule details defined variously.

Ba—Chinese word for "eight."

Babcock, Joseph P.—The American businessman who popularized the game of mah-jongg (giving it the name "mah-jongg") in the Western world in 1920.

Bai—Chinese name for the White Dragon tile; means "blank."

Bakelite—A type of plastic that was popular in the early twentieth century, used to manufacture radios and mah-jongg racks.

Balls—Alternate name for the suit of Dots.

Bamboo—(1) One of the three suits in mah-jongg; usually referred to as "Bams." (2) Material that was often used to make mah-jongg tiles in the early twentieth century (some modern sets are still made with bamboo backs).

Bao—Chinese term. Some forms of mahjong penalize a discarder who discards unwisely, especially when the resulting win is a high-scoring hand or special hand. Some American players call this "paying for the party."

Bettor—American game. (1) A fifth player who participates in a game by betting on who will win. (2) A term used by American players to refer to a wind indicator, used by some betting players to indicate which player she thinks will win.

Bionic—Alternate name for "Atomic."

Bird—Nickname for the One Bam tile, which usually depicts a sparrow, a peacock, or other bird.

Blank Tiles—Originally, White Dragon tiles were all blank. When plastic began to be used to make solid tiles, a rectangular design had to be added so players could distinguish the front from the back. Some modern sets come with blanks in case a tile is lost (then the blank can be marked as needed).

Blind Pass—American game. A practice optionally used in the Charleston when a player cannot comfortably pass three tiles.

Breaking the Wall—Dice are used in all forms of mah-jongg to determine where in the wall the deal is to begin; done to prevent cheating.

C—A symbol used on the American card to indicate that the so-marked hand must remain concealed until the player surprises everyone by declaring mah-jongg.

Call—To verbalize the intent to take a discard, for exposure or for mah-jongg.

Calling, On Call—To be in a ready state, waiting for a final tile to declare mah-jongg.

Card—American game. The yearly list of permissible hands, issued by the National Mah Jongg League.

Case—(1) A container in which the mah-jongg set is stored and carried. (2) The last tile of its kind. ("The player won on the case Three Dot tile.")

Catalin—A type of plastic formerly used to make mah-jongg tiles.

Characters—One of the three suits in mah-jongg. Also called "Ten Thousand," "Craks," and "Wan."

Charleston—American game. An intricate "dance" performed by the players at the beginning of each hand. Named for a dance that was popular during the Roaring Twenties, when the game of mah-jongg first became popular.

Chi—Chinese Official game. Chinese word for "seven"; Japanese word for "chow."

Chicken Hand—Chinese Official game. A hand that (were it not for the fact that it's valued at 8 points) would be worth 0 points, since it has no valuable pungs, no valuable patterns, and is not won with any kind of unique wait.

China Majiang Championship (CMC)—Chinese Official game. A Chinese nationwide tournament using the Chinese Official rules.

China Majiang Championship and Forum (CMCF)—The 2005 event, which was not only a tournament but also a meeting of world mahjong leaders.

Chinese Classical Mah-Jongg—The first well-documented variant of mah-jongg circa 1920. Since the advent of the American game and the Chinese Official rules, a variant that is no longer widely played.

Chinese Mah-Jongg Contest Rules—English translation of the title of the first official Chinese-language rule book for the Chinese Official game, printed in 1998.

Chinese Official Mahjong—A pattern-based variant of mahjong, used since 2002 in international championship tournaments.

Chips—Colorful circular plastic pieces, sometimes with holes in the center, used in lieu of money for scoring purposes. See also "Sticks."

Chow—Chinese Official game. Both a verb and a noun when used by English-speaking players. Noun: A sequential set of three single numbered tiles in the same suit. Verb: To claim a tile discarded by the upper player to form a sequential set of three single numbered tiles in the same suit. Chinese:

"chi pai." Interestingly, the term "chow" is slang for "eat"—which is what a player is said to do when "fed" a discard and subsequently chows it.

Chung—Chinese word for "Red Dragon tile." *Chung* means "center," and is the national symbol of China (China being the center of the world, to the Chinese).

Chur—Chinese; means "chow."

Circles—One of the three suits in mah-jongg. Also called "Dots," *"Tung,"* or *"Bing."*

Claim—To verbalize the intent to take a discarded tile, for exposure or for mah-jongg.

Clean Hand—Chinese Official game. Alternate name for "Half Flush." Also, "Clear Hand," "Cleared Hand."

Closed Hand—A hand that is revealed to the other players only upon declaration of mah-jongg. Also called "Concealed."

CMC—China Majiang Championship.

CMCF—China Majiang Championship and Forum.

Cold Wall—An unofficial table rule used by some players of American mah-jongg. Details of the rule vary at the whim of those using it. Players are usually prohibited from discarding a hot tile at a certain point near the end of the hand.

Color-Coding—American game. A system of using colored inks to represent the number of different suits that may be used to make a hand on the yearly card.

Combinatorics—A branch of mathematics devoted to the study of odds and probability, especially applicable to games involving numerous playing pieces or cards. Useful in strategy, for those who are mathematically oriented. (Slight play on words there.)

Concealed Hand—A hand that is revealed to the other players only upon declaration of mah-jongg. Also called "Closed."

Concealed Kong—Chinese Official game. When holding a complete set of 4 identical tiles within the hand, it's usually necessary to declare the kong in order to repair the tile count. The player is then permitted to place the 4 tiles facedown among his melds.

Conflicting Claims—It sometimes happens that multiple players claim a discarded tile. There are rules governing how such conflicting claims are to be handled.

Consecutive Run—American game. The middle section of the middle pane of the card, listing hands with consecutive sets of numbered suit tiles.

Corresponding Dragons—American game. Dragon tiles correspond to the suits. Red Dragon is considered to be the tenth or zeroth tile of the suit of Craks; Green Dragon is considered to be the tenth or zeroth tile of the suit of Bams; White Dragon is considered to be the tenth or zeroth tile of the suit of Dots.

Counters—Term used by some people to refer collectively to "chips" and "sticks."

Courtesy Pass—American game. The last move in the dance called the Charleston, after six passes, in which a player exchanges from 1 to 3 tiles with her opposite.

Craks—One of the three suits in a mah-jongg set. Short for "Characters," another name by which the suit is known. The red Chinese character at the bottom of each Crak tile means "Ten Thousand." The Chinese call this suit "Wan."

Curtsey or Curtsy—American game. A player serves out her wall, angling it in to the center of the table for the convenience of all players.

Daily Double—American game. Optional unofficial table rule in which the score is doubled when the dice total the same number as the first roll of the dice in a game session.

Dangerous Tile—A tile that might give an opponent a win. Defined variously.

Dead—In the American game, certain errors or circumstances result in a player being declared Dead (the dead player must stop playing). In the Chinese Official game, certain errors result in a player being penalized by being prohibited from declaring mahjong (the dead player must continue playing).

Dealer—The player sitting in the East seat at the beginning of a hand. This player rolls dice to determine where the wall is to be broken, and begins the process of taking tiles from the wall.

Declare—To verbalize the intent to take a discard, for exposure or for mah-jongg.

Declared Kong—Chinese Official game. A type of meld made when a player has a pung concealed within the hand and calls a discard to make an exposed kong.

Discard—A tile removed from the hand and placed in the center of the table, ending a player's turn.

Disorderly Discards—American game. Discards are placed randomly and haphazardly within the discard floor.

Dogging—The practice of discarding wanted tiles intentionally, usually near the end of a hand, in order to play defensively and prevent another player from winning.

Dong—Chinese word for "East Wind tile."

Dots—One of the three suits in mah-jongg. Also called "Circles," "*Tung*," and "*Bing*."

Double East—Chinese Official game. The dealer during the East round. This player is sitting in the East seat, and it's the East round, so if the player completes the hand with a pung of East, player earns extra points for "Double East."

Double Dice—American game. An unofficial table rule in which the winner will receive double score if the dice come up showing the same number on both dice.

Down—American game. When a discard has either been fully named by the discarder or touched to the table, it is considered "down," closing the window of opportunity for that player to change her mind and take the discard back into the hand. Also, when a joker has been discarded, it is considered "down," and nobody may claim it or use it in any way. "Down is dead."

Dragons—Name used in English to refer to the three nonwind honor tiles (red, green, white, AKA *chung, fa, bai*).

Draw—Both a verb and a noun. Verb: To pick a tile from the end of the wall. Noun: A hand that was not won by anyone. Also called a "Draw Game."

East—Used in several ways in mah-jongg. (1) One of the four Wind tiles. (2) The seat in which the dealer is sitting (also used to refer to the dealer herself). (3) The first round in a Chinese Official game.

Ee—Chinese word for "one."

Empty Call—To verbalize the intent to take a discard, then change one's mind and not take it after all. A punishable act in the Chinese Official game.

Er—Chinese word for "two." Pronounced "ur" or "ar."

Even Winds—American game. East and West are sometimes associated with even-numbered suit tiles.

Exchange—American game: alternate term sometimes used for "Redeem."

Exposed hand—American game. A hand whose sets are permitted to be melded prior to the declaration of mah-jongg.

Exposure—(1) A set of tiles (chow, pung, kong, quint, sextet, etc.) that has been melded prior to the declaration of mah-jongg. (2) The act of having exposed a set.

Fa—Chinese name for the Green Dragon tile; means "get rich."

False Declaration, False Mah-Jongg—Errors in declaring a win. A common error in American mah-jongg is to misread the card, and make the hand using the wrong combination of suits ("Maj in Error"). A common error in Chinese Official mahjong is to make a hand that doesn't earn the required 8 points.

Fan—Chinese word used in reference to the 81 scoring elements. When pluralized, no "s" is added ("There are 81 *fan* in the Chinese Official game.") Pronounced "fahn" (rhymes with "bonbon").

Farklempt—See "Verklempt."

Feed—To discard a tile which someone else can use, for a chow or, especially, for a win.

Fishing—Alternate term for "Calling."

Floor—The area in the center of the table where discards are placed.

Flower—A type of tile used in mah-jongg. Games that use flowers usually include 8 flowers (rather than 4). Flower tiles may depict flowers, people, objects, or animals, and may be labeled with flower names, season names, or other Chinese writing. In both American and Chinese Official mahjong, the numbers on the flower tiles (if present) have no meaning and may be ignored.

Flower Replacement—Chinese Official game. Flowers are not used in the hand, but instead are used to earn additional points upon winning. Flowers are usually melded immediately, necessitating the drawing of a replacement tile from the back end of the wall.

Frish—American game. Optional table rule under which a player may request a redeal.

Full Flush—Chinese Official game. A hand in which all the tiles are of the same suit.

Fully Concealed Hand—A hand with no pre-win exposures, won by self-pick.

Future—American game. An unofficial table rule in which players pick from the wall after discarding, rather than after the previous player has discarded. Used under the belief that it makes the game go faster. Because of problems that arose from this practice, it was specifically outlawed by the NMJL in 1956. Also called "Picking Ahead." See also "Looking Ahead."

Game—In American mah-jongg: One hand. Each play process that follows after a deal constitutes "a game." In Chinese mah-jongg: Four rounds (sixteen hands).

Game Session—In American mah-jongg: The entire time from the arrival of the players and starting play, up to the time players depart and go home. Usually three or four hours. In Chinese Official mahjong: A game session ends when either four rounds (sixteen hands) have been played, or the tournament "stop playing" gong has sounded, whichever occurs first. Usually 90 minutes or 2 hours (as determined by the tournament organizers). Chinese term is "*ju*."

Gang—Chinese for "kong."

Go-Around—Four turns not interrupted by anyone claiming a discard and disrupting the order of play. Four players, in turn, pick and discard a tile, during one normal "go-around." Chinese term is "*lun*."

Go Pie—American game. Most American players play for a purse of $5 or $3 or $10 in coins. This purse represents the maximum amount that a player can lose during the game session. When a player's purse contains no further coins, she is said to have "gone pie."

Go to the Wall—Alternate term for "Wall Game."

Great Wall—See "Wall."

Green Bams—The 2, 3, 4, 6, and 8 tiles in the suit of Bams.

Green Dragon—One of the nonwind honor tiles in mah-jongg. Chinese name is "*fa*" ("fortune").

Grouping—Term sometimes used to refer to a chow, pung, kong, quint, sextet, and sometimes a pair. "Set."

Half Flush—Chinese Official game. A hand in which tiles of two of the three suits are not present, and tiles of the third suit are present, together with honor tiles.

Hand—Noun used in two ways: (1) 13 or 14 tiles held by one player in a game of mah-jongg. (2) That portion of a mah-jongg game that consists of the deal, the playing, and someone winning (or not). Chinese term is "*pan*." American players call this a "game."

Honors—Collective term for the wind tiles (E, S, W, N) and the dragon tiles ("R," "G," "Wh").

Hop Toi—On those occasions when the dealer takes his or her last two tiles ("one and three"), and one tile is on one wall and the other tile is on another wall, some players say "*hop toi*" when taking them. It's a superstitious practice, done in the hopes of picking a pair of jokers (American game).

Hot Tile—A tile that might give an opponent the win. Variously defined.

Hot Wall—American game. An unofficial table rule under which a player who discards a hot tile and gives the win is penalized. The users of the table rule have to define the penalty and what exactly constitutes a hot tile.

House Rules—Alternate term for "Table Rules."

Hu—Chinese game; means "I win."

Hua, Hwar—Chinese game; means "Flower."

Identical Chows—Two or more chows in the same suit using the exact same numbers.

Indices—Numbers or letters (Arabic numerals as used in the West, and Roman letters as used in the West), placed on the face of a tile for the benefit of players who cannot read Chinese or who cannot be bothered to count the Dots or Bams on the face of the tile.

Ivory—Bonelike material made from the tusks of elephants or walruses. Formerly used to make mah-jongg tiles. More valuable material than bone. Now illegal to import into the United States, since elephants are an endangered species.

Joh—Chinese word for "nine."

Joker—American game. A tile used as a "wild tile." Jokers may represent any other tile (suit tile, wind tile, dragon tile, or flower), but only in pungs, kongs, quints, or higher (never in a pair or to represent a single).

Jokerless—American game. A hand made without any jokers.

Ju—Chinese game. See "Game Session."

Kaput—A Yiddish term meaning "finished," but not in the good way. Used for a hand or game that is or was lost. Example: "'My hand was kaput,' she kvetched."

Kards—American game. A term used in reference to paper mah-jongg cards that may be used in place of heavy tiles, usually when traveling. Spelled with a "k" to differentiate the deck from the NMJL card used by players of the American game.

KFC—Chinese game. Slang for "chicken hand."

Kitty—American game. Some players use a table rule in which players pay a small amount into a small bowl or cup when a wall game occurs. Also called a "pot" or "pishke."

Knitted Chow—Chinese Official game. A type of chow in which each of the 3 tiles is from a different suit.

Knitted Pung—A type of pung in which each of the 3 tiles is from a different suit. Not used in American or Chinese Official mahjong.

Knitted Set—Chinese Official game. Three tiles of a Knitted Straight, all of which belong to the same suit: 1-4-7, 2-5-8, or 3-6-9.

Knitted Straight—Chinese Official game. A full straight from 1 to 9, made of three Knitted Chows. In a proper Knitted Straight, the tiles of the three Knitted Chows can be rearranged to make three Knitted Sets. (The order of the suits in each chow correspond exactly to the order of the suits in the other chows.)

Kong—A set of 4 identical tiles. In American mah-jongg, any or all of the tiles in a kong may be jokers. Chinese term is *"gang."*

Kong Replacement—Chinese Official game. The usual hand consists of four sets and a pair, and the usual tile count of a hand is 14 tiles. When one of the sets is four of a kind, that equation goes out the window. So the player must take a replacement tile from the back end of the wall whenever making a kong.

Kvetch—American game. To complain. A popular pastime among players of the American game. Etymology: Yiddish. Example: "'Oy, I schlepped this mah-jongg case the whole two blocks over here, and I'm schvitzing like you wouldn't believe,' she kvetched."

Lai!—Chinese; means "Take your turn, already!"

Leung—Chinese term; means "dragon." Not used in reference to what Westerners call a dragon tile but rather to what Westerners call a straight (a sequence of number tiles from 1 to 9).

Like Numbers—Same-number tiles of different suits.

Like Tiles—Tiles that are alike one another. Defined herein because the question is frequently asked.

Liu—Chinese word for "six."

Looking Ahead—American game. Term applies to the outlawed table rule called "Futures" or "Picking Ahead." Players pick immediately after discarding but are not supposed to look at the tile until it's the player's turn.

Lower Seat—Chinese game. The player who goes after you in the order of play (the player on your right).

Luck—Preferred term: "Chance."

Lun—Chinese term. See "Go-Around."

Mah Que—The original name of the game before Joseph P. Babcock named it "mah-jongg."

Mah-Jongg—The name given the game by Joseph P. Babcock in 1920. Other spellings are acceptable as well (with or without the hyphen, and with or without the second G). American players pronounce the name with a soft J ("zh" sound); Asian players pronounce it with a hard J.

Maj—American nickname for "mah-jongg." Sometimes: "Mahj." Pronounced with a soft J ("zh" sound).

Majiang—Chinese way of writing "mah-jongg." Pronounced with a hard J.

Maj in Error—See "False Declaration, False Mah-Jongg."

Mei Yo or *Mei Yo Hua*—Chinese; means "I don't have any flowers."

Meld—A set of tiles laid down on the table or atop the rack after taking a discard to complete a set.

Menzen—Chinese; means "concealed."

Ming Toi—see *"Hop Toi."*

Mish—American game. An unofficial table rule. After the Charleston, players may pool their unwanted tiles, mix them up, and refill the hand from the pool. A fairly pointless exercise.

Mixed—Comprised of numerous suits.

Mixed Straight—Chinese game. A straight (1 to 9) made of three different-suited chows: 1-2-3 in one suit, 4-5-6 in a second suit, and 7-8-9 in the third suit.

Nan—Chinese word for "south."

National Mah Jongg League (NMJL)—The governing body of American mah-jongg, founded in 1937.

Natural—American game. A nonjoker tile, or a set (grouping) devoid of jokers. When an entire hand is made without jokers, it's called "jokerless."

Neutral—American game. "Suitless."

NEWS—American game. One of each wind tile. In hands calling for a NEWS, the grouping is not exposable, and jokers may not be used. Such a grouping is not a kong; it's four singles. Term may sometimes be used to refer to a hand made with such a grouping, or made from the Winds-Dragons section of the NMJL card.

Ninefold—American game. A set of nine identical tiles. Jokers are obviously necessary to make such a set. Currently not in use by the NMJL.

North—One of the four wind tiles. In the Chinese game, the player to the left of the dealer, or the fourth round of a game.

Obligatory Discard—Chinese game. When a tile from the player's hand has been accidentally revealed, the player is required to discard the tile on the next opportunity.

Octet, Octette—American game. A set of 8 identical tiles. Jokers are obviously necessary to make such a set. Currently not in use by the NMJL.

Odd Winds—American game. The winds N and S are sometimes associated with odd numbered tiles on the NMJL card.

OEMC—Open European Mahjong Championship. A recurring tournament using the Chinese Official rules.

One and Three—The last two tiles taken by the dealer; the tile atop the first stack, and the tile atop the third stack, of the wall.

One Bird—Alternate name for the "One Bam" tile.

13579—American game. The name of the bottom middle section of the NMJL card, whose hands are made from odd-numbered suit tiles (and sometimes dragons and flowers).

One Way Call—A state of readiness in which the waiting player needs one particular tile to win.

Opening the Wall—Alternate term for "Breaking the Wall."

Opposite—The player sitting directly across from the player under discussion.

Opposite Dragon—American game. A dragon tile not belonging to the one or two suits utilized in the rest of the hand.

Orderly Discards—Chinese Official game. Players are obliged to arrange their discards in rows of six, left to right, starting nearer the middle of the table, with subsequent rows farther from the middle of the table.

Original East—Chinese Official game. The player who acted as dealer at the beginning of the game. Equivalent to the "pivot" in American mah-jongg.

Out, Going Out—Term sometimes used for winning (making mah-jongg).

Own Wind—Chinese Official game. The wind tile corresponding to the player's seat position.

Oy, Oy vay—American game. An expression of dismay. Etymology: Yiddish. Cantonese equivalent: "Ayah!" American English equivalents: "Sheesh!" or "Whew!" or "Geez!"

Pai—Chinese; means "tile." Pronounced "pie."

Pair—Two identical tiles.

Pair Hand—A hand composed entirely of seven pairs.

Pan—Chinese term. That portion of a mahjong game that consists of the deal, the playing, and someone winning (or not). A "hand."

Pass—American game. One step in the Charleston, usually consisting of 3 tiles.

Pay for the Party—American game. Some players may use a table rule in which a player who discards a hot tile, giving the win, must pay for everyone. Chinese term: *"bao."*

Pei—Chinese; means "north."

Peng—Chinese. Pronounced "pung." See "Pung."

Pick—To take a tile from the wall.

Picking Ahead—American game. Unofficial (outlawed) table rule. Taking a tile from the wall immediately after discarding, rather than after the previous player has discarded.

Pie—See "Go Pie."

Pin Hu—Chinese Official game. A hand composed of all chows, with a nonhonor pair.

Pishke—American game. "Kitty."

Pivot—American game. The first dealer of the game session (usually the hostess), upon whose subsequent deals a seat rotation takes place.

Player—Any player seated at the table, especially someone who is not the dealer.

Player Wall—That portion of the wall that is directly in front of a player seated at the table.

Plotz—American game. To faint from excessive bad luck or good luck, or to burst with excessive excitement.

Po—Chinese; means "white."

Pot—American game. "Kitty."

Prevalent Wind, Prevailing Wind—Chinese Official game. The wind tile corresponding to the wind of the current round.

Promoted Kong—Chinese Official game. A kong made by adding a self-picked fourth tile to a previously melded pung.

Pung—Chinese Official game. English-speaking players use the term as both a noun and a verb. Noun: A set of three identical tiles. Verb: To claim a discard to meld an exposed set of three identical tiles. Chinese: *"peng pai."*

Pung Pung Hu (*Peng Peng Hu*)—Chinese. Meaning: "All Pungs."

Pure Hand—Chinese game. Alternate term for "Full Flush."

Pure Straight—Chinese game. A sequence from 1 to 9, consisting of three chows (1-2-3, 4-5-6, and 7-8-9), all in one suit.

Quan—Chinese. See "Round."

Quint—American game. Five identical tiles. Unless it's a quint of flower tiles, at least one joker must be used.

Rack—A multipurpose device used by non-Asian players. Used to make straight walls, to display the hand to the player while concealing it from others, and to display melds. Many racks also are useful for storing chips, although most American players do not use the chips, preferring to play for coins.

Raw Tile—A tile that has not previously been discarded or exposed.

Ready—A state of waiting for one tile to complete the hand and win.

Red Dragon—One of the three nonwind honor tiles. See *"Chung."*

Redeeming a Joker—American game. A practice by which a player may exchange a natural tile for an exposed joker.

Reverse Counting—After rolling the dice, the normal practice is to count the tiles of the wall from right to left. But experienced players, upon rolling a high number like 10, 11, or 12, prefer to count the wall tiles from the left end, knowing that the wall is nineteen stacks long (American game) or eighteen stacks long (Chinese game). When rolling a 12, it's faster to count

7 from the left (American) or 6 from the left (Chinese) than to count 12 from the right.

Reversible Tiles—Chinese game. Tiles that appear the same, regardless of whether they're right side up or upside down (disregarding the indices, if present). The reversible tiles are the 1, 2, 3, 4, 5, 8, and 9 of Dots, the 2, 4, 5, 6, 8, and 9 of Bams, and the White Dragon.

Robbing the Kong—Chinese game. A ready/waiting player is permitted to go out on a tile that an opponent uses to promote a kong. Considered win by discard.

Rotation—See "Seat Rotation."

Round—Chinese game. One-fourth of a game. The interval during which all four players have acted as dealer. Chinese: "*quan.*"

Round Wind—See "Prevalent Wind."

Safe Tile—A tile that is unlikely to be wanted by an opponent for mah-jongg. Opposite of "hot tile."

San—Chinese; means "three."

Schlep, Shlep—American game. (1) To labor mightily at transporting a heavy mah-jongg case to the home of another player. (2) Any arduous journey, usually involving carrying heavy items. Etymology: Yiddish.

Schmutz—Dirt, grime, anything that might dirty a mah-jongg tile or table. German word used in Yiddish, so term may be heard in a game of American mah-jongg.

Schvitz—Yiddish: to sweat. Something one does when schlepping.

Seasons—A type of flower tile upon which is written (in either Chinese or English abbreviations) the names of the four seasons.

Seat Rotation—The practice of switching player seats to mix up the playing order. In the American game, it's done out of a superstitious belief that some seats are luckier than others. In the Chinese game, it's done for strategic reasons (to change the feeding order).

Seat Wind—The wind tile that corresponds to the player's seat position.

Self-Pick—One of the two ways of winning (the other being to win by discard).

Septet, Septette—American game. A set of seven identical tiles. Unless the set consists of flowers, jokers are obviously necessary to make such a set. Currently septettes and higher are not in use by the NMJL.

Serve the Wall—American game. Alternate name for the "Curtsey." A player pushes out her wall, angling it in to the center of the table for the convenience of all players.

Set—(1) Term used to refer to exposable groupings of tiles: chows, pungs, kongs, quints, etc. (2) Term used to refer collectively to the tabletop equipment for playing mah-jongg (all the tiles, dice, chips, racks, and the wind indicator, if present).

Sextet, Sextette—American game. A set of six identical tiles. Unless the set consists of flowers, jokers are obviously necessary to make such a set.

Shih (Shuh)—Chinese word for "ten."

Sih (Suh)—Chinese word for "four."

Similar Chows—Chinese game. Chows composed of the same numerical sequence but made from different suits. Alternate name for "Mixed Double Chow."

Similar Pungs—Pungs composed of the same number but made from different suits. In the Chinese Official game: "Double Pung."

Simples—Nonterminal suit tiles: suit tiles numbered 2 through 8.

Singles And Pairs—American game. The lower right section of the NMJL card, in which no hand uses pungs, kongs, quints, or sextets, and in which jokers may not be used.

Singleton—A single tile (a tile without any mates, which is not part of any set).

Skill—That attribute that comes to a player after much practice and with much thought; an attribute that outweighs mere "chance" in the long run.

Soap—American nickname for White Dragon. So called because originally, White Dragon tiles were blank tiles made of bone, resembling small bars of soap.

South—One of the four wind tiles. In the Chinese game, the player to the right of the dealer, or the second round of a game.

Stealing—American game. Unofficial (incorrect) term for the "Blind Pass."

Sticks—(1) Long slim pieces made of bone or plastic, painted with patterns of dots and used as chips. (2) Nickname for the suit of Bamboo.

Straight—A sequence of suit tiles from 1 to 9.

Strategy—The application of planned action, intended to increase the chances of winning or to decrease one's probable losses.

Suit—A family or "type" of mah-jongg tile distinguished by being similarly marked, either with Dots (circles), bamboo sticks (the ace or one being usually marked with a bird instead), or Chinese numbers (multiples of ten thousand).

Suitless—American game. Flowers and wind tiles do not belong to any suit, thus are neutral or "suitless." Although the dragon tiles are considered to belong to a suit (red with Craks, green with Bams, white with Dots), there is a special use for the White Dragon, as zero in numerical groupings (such as 2007, 2008, 2009, 2010, 10, 20, etc.). In such numerical groupings, the White Dragon is considered as no longer belonging to any suit. Thus, it is "suitless" (neutral, not aligned with any suit).

Symbol Tile—American game. A nonjoker tile (another name for "natural tile").

Table Rule—A special rule or interpretation of the rules, not in accordance with the standard or official rules. A common practice among players of American mah-jongg.

Tail—American game. An optional method of setting up the wall. Because American racks are often shorter than the nineteen-stack walls, some players take the extra tiles and arrange them into a short "tail."

Take—Term used to refer to the use of a discard (as opposed to picking a tile from the wall).

Tchotchkes—Yiddish word that means knick-knacks, doodads, or thingamabobs.

Tell—Noun. Borrowed here from poker. The characteristic mannerism, body language, or gesture(s) made by a player who is ready for mah-jongg; the "giveaway signal" that you shouldn't discard her ready tile. "I saw him raise his left eyebrow; that's his tell."

Ten Thousand—Alternate name for the suit of Craks (Characters).

Terminals—Those suit tiles numbered 1 and 9.

369—American game. The middle right section of the card, depicting hands using tiles numbered 3, 6, and 9 only (and sometimes dragons or flowers).

Throw—Alternate term for "Discard."

Tiao—Chinese name for the suit of Bamboo. Pronounced "tyow."

Tile Count—The proper tile count of a mah-jongg hand between turns is 13 (in the Chinese game, ignore flowers and the fourth tile of any kongs), and during turns 14. The proper tile count of a mah-jongg set is 144 (Chinese game) or 152 (American game).

Tile Names—The names of the tiles in American English and in Chinese:

Tile	American	Chinese	Tile	American	Chinese
	One Dot	Ee Tung		One Crak	Ee Wan
	Two Dot	Ur Tung		Two Crak	Ur Wan
	Three Dot	San Tung		Three Crak	San Wan
	Four Dot	Suh Tung		Four Crak	Suh Wan
	Five Dot	Wuu Tung		Five Crak	Wuu Wan
	Six Dot	Liu Tung		Six Crak	Liu Wan
	Seven Dot	Chee Tung		Seven Crak	Chee Wan
	Eight Dot	Ba Tung		Eight Crak	Ba Wan
	Nine Dot	Joh Tung		Nine Crak	Joh Wan
	One Bam	Ee Tiao		East	Dong
	Two Bam	Ur Tiao		South	Nan
	Three Bam	San Tiao		West	Si
	Four Bam	Suh Tiao		North	Pei
	Five Bam	Wuu Tiao		White (Soap)	Bai (Baiban)
	Six Bam	Liu Tiao		Green	Fa
	Seven Bam	Chee Tiao		Red	Chung
	Eight Bam	Ba Tiao		Flower	Hua (Hwar)
	Nine Bam	Joh Tiao		Joker	

Notes:

1. The Chinese names are written the way they sound, as opposed to using an official Chinese transliteration system such as *pinyin*.
2. Alternative names or pronunciations for tiles are included in parentheses, where applicable.

Trades—A type of flower tile depicting people of various occupations or trades.

Triplet—Three identical tiles. Proper name: "Pung."

Trump—Term used in this book in reference to a circumstance that outweighs another. For example, a call for a discard to make mah-jongg always outweighs ("trumps") a call for the same discard to make a pung.

Tung—Chinese name for the suit of Dots (Circles). Pronounced "toong" (rhymes with "look").

Turn—The interval between (1) either the player's upper seat discards a tile or the player verbalizes an unopposed call for a discarded tile, and (2) the player declares mah-jongg or discards a tile.

2468—American game. The middle left section of the NMJL card, which lists hands made only with even-numbered suit tiles (and sometimes flowers or dragons).

200x—American game. Term used in this book to refer to any tile grouping representing a year of the first decade of the twenty-first century (2005, 2006, 2007, 2008, etc.). A grouping made of two single tiles and a pair, in which jokers may not be used. Year hands are always listed in the upper left section of the NMJL card.

201x—American game. Term used in this book to refer to any tile grouping representing a year of the second decade of the twenty-first century (2010, 2011, 2012, etc.). A grouping made of single tiles, thus jokers may not be used.

Upper Seat—The player whose turn precedes the turn of the player under discussion (the player seated to the left of the player under discussion). In Chinese mahjong, one's upper seat can "feed" the player chowable tiles.

Verklempt—American game. A state of being "all choked up," perhaps from happiness or sadness. Could result from either an extremely bad night or an extremely good night at mah-jongg. Also "Farklempt."

Waiting—The state of being ready for mah-jongg, needing one tile to win.

Wall—The two-tile-high line of tiles arranged around the table in a square.

Wall Game—A hand that was won by nobody. Also called a "Draw."

Wan—Chinese; means "Ten Thousand." Name of one of the three suits in mahjong.

West—One of the four wind tiles. In the Chinese game, the player seated opposite the dealer, or the third round of a game.

Western Indices—Markings (Arabic numerals and Roman letters) added to mah-jongg tiles for the benefit of players who cannot read Chinese or cannot be bothered to count the pips on a suit tile.

Wind Indicator, Wind Marker—A device included with some mah-jongg sets, used to indicate the current round wind. American players call the device a "bettor."

Window of Opportunity—The brief interval of time in which a player may call for a discard. American game: The window closes when the next player racks or discards. Chinese game: The window closes 3 seconds after the tile was discarded.

Winds—The nondragon honor tiles. Also used in reference to the seat positions and the names of the rounds in a Chinese game.

Winds-Dragons—American game. The upper right section of the NMJL card, listing hands consisting of honor tiles (and sometimes flowers, or odd or even suit tiles).

World Mahjong Competition Rules (WMCR)—Alternate name for Chinese Official Mahjong.

World Mahjong Competition Committee (WMCC)—The governing body of Chinese Official Mahjong. Other names may also be used, at the whim of the translator or the governing body itself. For example: World Mahjong Organization (WMO).

Wu—Chinese word for "five."

Wu Men Chi—Chinese; means "five types" (the All Types hand).

Wu-tzu—Chinese: "No honors."

X—American game. A symbol used on the NMJL card to indicate that it is permissible to make exposures in the so-marked hand prior to declaring mahjongg.

Xi—Chinese word for "west." Pronounced "see."

Zero—American game. The White Dragon tile is used to represent zero in certain hands.

Zimo—Chinese; means "pick."

APPENDIX 7
Chinese Official Mahjong Scoring at a Glance

Chinese Official Mahjong Scoring at a Glance

Category		Points	88	64	48	32	24
Honor Tile Based			Big Four Winds Big Three Dragons	Little Four Winds Little Three Dragons All Honors			
Chow Based	One-Step-Up Hands					Four Shifted Chows	
	Chow Hands				Quadruple Chow		Pure Triple Chow
	Straight Hands						
	Terminal Hands			Pure Terminal Chows			
Pung Based	Pung Hands			All Terminals Four Concealed Pungs	Four Shifted Pungs	All Terminals & Honors	All Even Pure Shifted Pungs
	Kong Hands		Four Kongs			Three Kongs	
Seven Pairs Hands			Seven Shifted Pairs				Seven Pairs
Suit Based			All Green Nine Gates				Full Flush
Terminal Based							Upper Tiles Middle Tiles Lower Tiles
Knitted Tiles Based							Greater Honors & Knitted Tiles
Types of Wait							
Special Hands			Thirteen Orphans				

16	12	8	6	4	2	1
	Big Three Winds		Two Dragons		Dragon Pung Prevalent Wind Seat Wind	
Pure Shifted Chows			Mixed Shifted Chows			
		Mixed Triple Chow			All Chows	Pure Double Chow Mixed Double Chow
Pure Straight	Knitted Straight	Mixed Straight				Short Straight
Three-Suited Terminal Chows						Two Terminal Chows
Triple Pung Three Concealed Pungs		Mixed Shifted Pungs	All Pungs		Double Pung Two Concealed Pungs	Pung of Terminals or Honors
		Two Concealed Kongs	One Melded & One Concealed	Two Melded Kongs	Concealed Kong	Melded Kong
			Half Flush All Types			One Voided Suit No Honors
All Fives	Upper Four Lower Four			Outside Hand	All Simples	
	Lesser Honors & Knitted Tiles					
		Last Tile Draw Last Tile Claim Out on Replacement Tile Robbing the Kong	Melded Hand	Fully Concealed Hand Last Tile	Concealed Hand	Edge Wait Closed Wait Single Wait Self-Drawn
		Reversible Tiles Chicken Hand			Tile Hog	Flower Tiles

INDEX